Life
Under the
Corporate
Microscope

A Maverick's Irreverent Perspective

Larry Underwood

Outskirts Press, Inc.
Denver, Colorado

Life Under the Corporate Microscope
A Maverick's Irreverent Perspective
All Rights Reserved.
Copyright © 2009 Larry Underwood
V3.0

Outskirts Press, Inc.
http://www.outskirtspress.com

ISBN: 978-1-4327-3393-3

Outskirts Press and the "OP" logo are trademarks belonging to Outskirts Press, Inc.

PRINTED IN THE UNITED STATES OF AMERICA

Acknowledgements

I'd like to thank Jack C Taylor for having the courage and vision to found the small leasing company, known as "Executive Leasing", in 1957.

To Wayne Kaufmann and Doug Brown, thanks for having the courage and vision to hire me in 1974.

To the rest of the corporate hierarchy at Enterprise Rent-a-Car; thanks for putting up with me for twenty-six years.

To the fine employees of the West Group while I was its General Manager, thanks for doing your jobs so well, making mine so much easier.

To my two wonderful kids (who are now adults), Justin and Taryn, thanks for putting up with me while I wrote this book, and for presumably, finally reading it.

Introduction

After graduating from an institution of higher learning called Rockford College in 1974, and returning back home to St Louis to marry my college sweetheart, I was fortunate enough to have hooked on with a building products supply company (Georgia Pacific) that would lay me off inside of four months.

Being young and naive, I never saw it coming, nor did I realize that being laid off was actually a blessing in disguise. The recession in the housing market, which led to my sudden unemployment created the perfect opportunity to start another random career, this time, in the car rental business, with a company called "Executive Leasing". I was hired, and stuck around for twenty-six years, while becoming one of its highest paid, and probably, most irreverent executives.

The company would change its name to Enterprise Rent-a-Car, and I would be embarking on a career that would pay me more money than I ever dreamed possible, in a business I truly loved. At the peak of my career, which happened to be my final year with Enterprise, I was raking in close to $4 million per year while overseeing one of the company's most profitable and fun-loving operations.

I retired after making it through the first year of the current millennium. By that time, the company that I loved had evolved into a humorless bureaucracy; not that there's anything wrong with that; but I clearly didn't fit in with that type of environment, so it was time to go, with no regrets; except of course, I wouldn't be making so much money.

The history of Enterprise, through my irreverent eyes, examines the remarkable transformation of a company that only leased cars for the first five years of its existence, started its rental division almost as an afterthought five years later, thus inadvertently going on to become the largest and most profitable car rental company in the world.

This book captures my perspective of the events that shaped Enterprise and profoundly affected not only countless careers, but personal lives as well. The observations I make are my honest opinion and may not be shared by others however please keep in mind that I'm usually right.

The company's success began with the simple, but not particularly "easy" goal of its founder, Jack C Taylor, to deliver the best customer service possible at all times; and remarkably has continued through the efforts of its front line employees, who so consistently; often thanklessly; take care of its customers, day in and day out. These are the people who work the hardest and typically get paid on the lower end of the spectrum. This book is dedicated to you. Hang in there. Someday, you may become a big shot.

After all, if it could happen to a guy like me, who never really took anything too seriously, it could happen to you.

Chapter 1

Paying Dues Paid Big Dividends

"Hi, Uncle Larry; I hear you party like a rock star!" My mind went blank when this young, blonde, voluptuous vixen who, also happened to be a newly hired management trainee introduced herself to me. Stunned, and feeling anything like a rock star at that particular moment, I cleverly replied; "Sure; nice to meet you. Uh."

I was however, quite impressed with the bold ice-breaking method she coyly employed to meet the big shot General Manager, who had long been labeled with that somewhat goofy but seemingly harmless nickname, "Uncle Larry"; as I continued stammering on, I kept trying to think of any rock stars who could possibly be more boring than me; to no avail.

Finally, I was rescued from my distracted conversation with this gorgeous new employee, as some of the other Fresno faithful made their way over to greet their fearless leader.

Ironically, her remark was a fairly accurate assessment of my reputation with the staunchly conservative car rental company in the late '90s; I was "Uncle Larry", the irreverent (generally vilified by the corporate hierarchy, revered by most of my employees) General

Manager of a mass of territory of locations in the west, known simply as the "West Group", and on this particular occasion, I happened to be in Fresno, paying a little visit to the troops in the field.

My career with Enterprise Rent-a-Car spanned twenty-six years (1974-2000), beginning when real rock stars like The Rolling Stones and Led Zeppelin were in their primes, and up and comers like Aerosmith and Queen were just getting recognition.

Over those twenty-six years, other rock stars gained notoriety, from The Ramones to The Red Hot Chili Peppers, from Beck to Pink, and from Cheryl Crowe to The Black Crowes.

Still pondering a vague comparison between my relatively tranquil lifestyle to just about any rock star on the planet, I concluded that I was generally out of their league.

No doubt, I was extremely well paid as a General Manager with Enterprise, but my idea of wild entertainment consisted of having a few beers after work and chasing women, a lifestyle that seemed socially acceptable for any middle-aged millionaire bachelor.

I never trashed a hotel room in my life, never partied with Hunter S Thompson, never drove a Ferrari 120 miles per hour down Sunset Boulevard, was never photographed by Annie Liebowitz for the cover of the "Rolling Stone", and certainly never had sex-crazed groupies throwing themselves at me; damn.

I did meet Wayne Newton, the entertainer who personified the post Elvis Las Vegas, as he was kind enough to attend an Enterprise function, celebrating the company's 40th anniversary; he even gave me his autograph: "To Uncle Larry; Best Wishes; Wayne Newton"

I also met Willie Nelson at charity golf tournament in Austin, Texas, as he rolled out of his pickup truck just in time to make his tee time, but that only entailed a brief "howdy" while he grinned at everybody there trying to look serious about their upcoming round; what a character; absolutely nothing fazed him.

But I still had fun living my subdued rock star lifestyle. Whenever I'd hit the road and visit one of the cities in my domain, I'd usually take a bunch of employees out with me to some bar and throw down a few, to discuss whatever relevant issues they may need to vent to their empathetic General Manager at the end of a long and arduous day.

I knew what it was like to start out at the bottom; everybody had to start out there to really understand the business; and the bottom at Enterprise was really pretty low; but in the long run, once you pay your dues, you'll understand it was the best way to prepare yourself for just about anything else the business threw at you.

Enterprise has had a long and glorious tradition of working their employees to death in hectic surroundings with lots of overtime to make them feel special, so on occasion, such as this particular visit to Fresno, I figured they could use a few cocktails after another grueling day in the trenches, to ease the trauma of maybe not having quite enough cars at their disposal, or having some pissed off customer absurdly complaining about trivial bullshit, such as the color of the Corolla they had just rented, and would only need for a day or two.

Little did I know that this beautiful blonde vixen who greeted me with such devilish ice-breaking enthusiasm, would soon leave the company for some reason or another, move to Phoenix; call me up one night, completely out of the blue, and we'd have a brief fling. It was certainly fun while it lasted.

Ironically, all this devilish fun began the night before the biggest annual meeting Enterprise had for General Managers like myself, the Fall Officers Meeting. This one, the 1998 version, just happened to be in Phoenix, and I happened to have a house in Phoenix (as well as Las Vegas, where my office was located). Obviously for me, I was in the right place at the right time.

That was one meeting I must've looked pretty happy attending, for sure. Usually, I hated meetings, primarily since they're generally a waste of time and money. Enterprise loved meetings.

Aside from the meetings, the life of a General Manager with Enterprise Rent-a-Car was great, particularly if you were one of those fortunate souls who began their Groups from scratch (as I did), ran it (quite) profitably (as I did), and was given the maximum commission available (as I got), along with the autonomy to run your Group the way you saw fit (which I had for most of the time). Those were definitely the good old days.

Those types of pay plans are pretty much obsolete nowadays (not to mention the autonomy), as the company became more fiscally prudent and stopped paying the upper management in a Group "top dollar" to manage its operation; usually "low to mid dollar" does the trick nowadays; in retrospect, it seems the company really had no idea what kind of monster they were creating when they devised those wonderful, incentive-based, original "top dollar" pay plans.

Enterprise simply grew so much larger and more profitable than anything ever imagined by any corporate guru, or non-corporate guru, for that matter. Actually, I don't think we had any gurus.

The unforeseen and relentless growth, which started around the time I became a General Manager, in the middle '80s inexorably continued, and by the early '90s Enterprise, the sleeping giant; the world's best kept car rental secret; not only surprised and surpassed Hertz for the top spot in the industry; it seemed Enterprise was the only company making huge amounts of profit, while most others didn't, and some lost so much money, they had to cease operations altogether.

By the beginning of the millennium, Enterprise Rent-a-Car, no longer a secret, was not only the number one car rental company in the world in terms of the number of cars it had in service, it typically raked in more profit each year than all the other car rental companies, combined.

By 2007, the most successful car rental company in history, acquired both Alamo and National, giving Enterprise the leading share of the air travel niche of the business, to go along with their already existing dominance in the local "home-city market".

Meanwhile, back in the '90s, the Officers of the company enjoying the rewards of this very successful and somewhat surprising explosion of profitable growth were now reaping the lucrative commissions from their efforts; millionaires were starting to emerge from nearly every well established Group; and quite a few of those millionaires soon became multi-millionaires.

Those unfortunate and ineffective General Managers who were unable to capitalize on the opportunity to make huge sums of money during those glorious years, which really started heating up in the late '80s and through most of the '90s, were usually sent packing.

Gradually, the old guard, with their pockets full of loot, began stepping aside, some more willingly than others.

Since I was generally regarded to be a notoriously irreverent old guard maverick, in addition to being on the dreaded highest commission pay plan allowed by Enterprise law (which filled my pockets with loot) to the company's bureaucratic upper echelon, the thought of me making millions each year surely rankled more than a few; in fact, some of the corporate drones would make snide remarks to me about my income level, as if I was some idiot who had just won a lottery, as opposed to a guy who was getting paid for performance.

The more money I made for the company, the more I made individually; it was the perfect Enterprise world, as far as I could tell.

Consequently, toward the end of my increasingly lucrative career, as much as I tried to go unnoticed, I just couldn't pull it off. They always knew what I was up to; and as far as the corporate hierarchy was concerned, with my income getting close to $4 million per year, and climbing, I was usually up to no good.

For the last four or five years of my career, I was constantly under the corporate microscope, and I was all too aware of that feeling. I knew it would only be a matter of time before something going on in the West Group, whether it be legitimate business issues, or personal issues aimed at attacking anything that seemed like a plausible flaw in my character, would be dissected so thoroughly, they'd have to find something wrong, real or imagined, sooner or later.

Of course, things didn't used to be that way.

As an entry-level employee in the rental department back in 1974, $650 a month was the going rate, and that didn't include overtime, which was a moot point, because as far as Executive Leasing Company (their maiden name) was concerned, overtime didn't exist. If an employee didn't like the hours and/or the pay; that's too bad; now go work someplace else. Hell, I just wanted a job, and that sounded like a reasonable pay plan to me, so I stayed put, as a 50 to 60 hour workweek seemed perfectly normal.

Of course, even in 1974, making only $650 per month and working all those hours seemed anything but "normal" to most normal people; but I didn't care, since I was anything but "normal" myself. I think I was nuts, but have no papers to prove it or anything; but that has to explain my tolerance for this kind of employment, which I calculated paid me almost two dollars per hour; not bad; not bad at all.

As it turned out the way they paid many overworked employees was, inevitably, against some kind of government wage law and the next thing you knew, Executive Leasing was in trouble but never admitted doing anything wrong.

It was amazing, but during the entire twenty-six years I was employed by Executive Leasing/Enterprise Leasing/ Enterprise Rent-a-Car, they never made a mistake, or if they did, said they didn't agree with the verdict, or whatever, and tried to make believe that we, the employees, really believed they never screwed up. To this day, the company that never made a mistake continues to find themselves in trouble over the way they pay some of their people, which after all of these years, seems more that a little bit mystifying; even though it's not their fault.

For the record, I have absolutely no problem with the way Enterprise paid me during the course of my employment with them, even when I was making two bucks an hour.

Also, for the record, I firmly believe Enterprise made no mistake when they hired me, because I actually did a pretty good job for them, and I don't really think I'm crazy, either (lovably zany, perhaps).

October 8, 1974, is when I inauspiciously launched a career which unbeknownst to me, would some day make me one of its highest paid executives, and I'm proud to say I never had to fill out one of those stupid fucking time cards in my entire career.

I had to take a $25 per month pay cut from what I had been making with Georgia Pacific, and the hours were brutal; but I didn't mind. I grew to love the job and figured I'd advance with the company in one way or the other. I had a very patient approach to my career, and never fretted over little things like dealing with tough management or how I'd make it to the next level. I just felt that something good would happen for me in due time; and sure enough, it did; and that's why I'm writing this book.

After being laid off from economically distressed Georgia Pacific, I was relieved to hear that Executive Leasing Company had never laid off a single employee in its illustrious seven-teen year history. That's the most significant thing I remember from the two interviews I had with Wayne Kaufmann and Doug Brown.

The rest of it went something like "blah, blah, blah, you'll need to get a haircut" and "blah, blah, blah, when you screw up just admit it" and "blah, blah, blah, we're going to work you to death."

Naturally, I agreed with everything these two guys were saying, and they both liked me enough to offer me a job, which I wisely accepted, reassured that at least I probably wouldn't be laid off this time. My thoughts went out to Georgia Pacific, hoping that the $675 they were saving each month, by laying me off, would return them to solvency.

The fact that I had no idea what my new job really entailed didn't bother me. I just wanted to get in the door and start receiving paychecks again. I could learn whatever I needed to learn with the good old-fashioned training program known as "Throw my ass in the fire".

After spending my first day on the job hanging out with Wayne Kaufmann, the unpretentious home spun head-honcho of daily rental, in the comfortable surroundings of Executive/Enterprise Leasing Company's headquarters (the company also had offices in Atlanta, Kansas City, Orlando, Tampa, Jacksonville, and had just opened Houston); a location that also housed an impressive looking rental and leasing facility, I thought to myself, "This is a great job. I haven't had to do anything yet."

Wayne even sent me home early that day, telling me that I'd need to report to the South Kingshighway branch the next day. That's when reality set in, and I'd actually have to work for a living, and this place somewhere in south St Louis is where I'd ultimately spend the first eighteen months of my career, although I was lucky I wasn't canned after the first day.

When you show up late on the very first day of work, your manager will tend to not like you. That's right, kids. Don't be late for work, especially on that first day; you're trying to make a good impression, and being late usually doesn't help accomplish that goal.

Unfortunately for me, that's exactly what happened; but the good news is I somehow survived this blatant act of what appeared to be total indifference to the job, because in reality, I wasn't indifferent at all. I was simply incompetent, which isn't so good either; but at least I cared.

I won't even bother with the excuse I had about being late, because I don't remember having a valid one. Walking into the office and saying something like, "Uh, the commute took longer than I expected blah, blah, blah" may cause the unfortunately logical reply, "Well, maybe you should've tried to get here an hour ahead of time, to allow for that unfortunate situation, don't you think blah?"

I learned my lesson, the hard way; and right off the bat; nobody seemed to like me; after all, I lacked the necessary foresight to do such complicated tasks as start my journey to work a little earlier, and that was understandable; I didn't even like me; however, I vowed I sure as hell was never going to be late to work again, and thought that maybe one day, blah, someone would like me, blah; they would really like me, blah.

To make a long story not quite as long, but certainly not short; my first manager, a guy I'll refer to as "Ed", probably thought I was a complete slacker (although that term hadn't come into vogue yet), and it took a while for him to get over that impression of me. I think it took him about a year to realize that I was an okay guy.

Enough about me; let's talk about Ed. Ed was an odd sort of fellow who was kind of funny looking in a general sort of "Cohen brothers" way. He looked like a cross between Richard Nixon and Steve Busceme; you know, that funny looking guy in "Fargo" and various other movies that required a funny looking guy. Since Nixon was kind of funny looking in a general sort of a shifty eyed, five o'clock shadowy way, the blend of the two generally funny looking men made for one funny looking Executive Leasing Company branch rental manager.

The fact that Ed looked and acted kind of funny didn't really bother me, though. Hell, I'm kind of funny looking too, in a Jim Carrey funny looking sort of way, although when I first started he would've only been twelve years old, so back then I just looked like an average, run of the mill, dork, complete with glasses and really bad hair.

What bothered me was his handwriting was so funny looking and illegible, I found it virtually impossible to actually read anything he wrote on a sheet of paper. Today, that wouldn't matter. Nobody writes anything by hand anymore. Back in the '70s, it was important to read shit that other people in the office wrote, such as those all important reservations, which told us who was coming in to rent a particular vehicle, and who would be paying the bill; otherwise everything would get all messed up, customers would be pissed, and nobody would ever get trained; like me, for example.

Needless to say, I hated that fucking job, initially, because I felt like this Ed guy was never going to learn how to write any more legibly than the shit he was already putting on paper with his shitty little pen because he was like thirty or something, and therefore too old to change his ways, and since he was my boss, that was going to make it difficult to advance to the next level, whatever that was.

I felt hopelessly lost, like I was in a really horrifying Twilight Zone episode, and it was freaking me out man; especially when I heard Rod Serling's narration:

"Submitted for your approval, Larry Underwood, a young, immature and dorky looking management trainee, unable to understand a fucking thing that his evasive and funny looking manager, known as 'Ed', is so desperately trying to communicate; to a punk-ass slacker who doesn't even have sense enough to show up for work on time.

Unfortunately for Larry, he would be trapped in a place far from the normal environment of work; a place of quiet rush hour desperation, where the incompetent Larry would always be late, and even when he does arrive, it really won't matter; because he'll never be able to read Ed's scribbling; the sign post ahead says, 'You're fucked, Larry'; have fun trying to get out of the Twilight Zone."

Luckily, I spent so much time driving customers around and going to the car wash, I didn't even need to be able to read to get by. I was so glad I got that fucking college diploma; too bad my wonderful Bachelor of Arts in Economics was of no practical use here in the

Twilight Zone. Also, to make my job seem even more demeaning, we weren't even called management trainees yet; we were "number three guys".

But wait; I'm an Underwood. I grew up in a dysfunctional broken home where everything abnormal is normal. I could handle this situation, so help me God.

Yes, my early days with the company started out a little bumpy; that's for sure. But I'm here to tell you, I made it; without any fancy training program and all that mumbo jumbo shit these young kids are getting today. I made it by being able to break the code on Ed's mysterious handwriting, to the point where I could comprehend over half of what was written, and by listening, very closely to everything that was said in that office, so I'd understand what was really going on.

I guess you could say I threw my ass into the fire, time and time again, and sure, I got burned, a lot, but I survived. What can I say? I'm just a lucky stiff who kind of took it upon myself to learn what was needed to not just "get by"; no, by God, I'd succeed, and eventually, I'd become the assistant manager of that very office, thanks to a little help from the previous assistant manager who decided to leave town, a guy I'll call "Bruce".

All kidding aside, those early days may have been confusing and even depressing at times, but I always believed that you've got to pay your dues before you can achieve any significant degree of success.

I never forgot what it was like to work in the trenches, clean those filthy cars in blazing summer heat, or dig those cars out of three feet of snow in the middle of January. And as much as we tried to please customers, it was impossible to please all of them. I've been yelled at, shoved, spit at, jabbed, threatened with bodily harm, and even had loose change thrown at my head (the customer owed me a fucking quarter and didn't want to pay).

I've had drunks, druggies, whores, con artists, deadbeats, and simple scumbags try to weasel their way into getting a car for free. Every now and then, they'd burn you for thousands of dollars of uncollected rental charges, or worse yet, get the car for keeps. Usually, we'd at least get our cars back. I've repossessed dozens of cars at all hours of the day or night. It was quite an adrenalin rush to track a car down that was feared lost forever, sneak in with an extra set of keys, and peal out of there; sometimes with the deadbeat chasing you down in his bathrobe and slippers in the middle of the night.

Those early days were mostly fun, primarily because the other employees in the office were cool to hang out with, except maybe Ed, either during work or afterwards, at a nearby tavern or on the softball field. We always found something to laugh about, and usually it was at our own expense.

In those days, the employees in the rental department were considered the red headed stepchildren of the company, the under dogs, the people least likely to succeed. I quickly discovered that the path to the top of the ladder was supposed to go through the leasing department.

That was Executive Leasing Company's original blue print for success, but there were those, like myself, who didn't think that was necessarily such a good idea.

Chapter 2

From Executive Leasing To Enterprise Rent-A-Car: The Blueprint For Success Is Revamped

It's hard to believe, but the car rental division of Executive Leasing, a company founded by the great Jack C Taylor in 1957, wasn't established until 1962. The primary reason Jack ventured into the car rental business was to take care of his lease customers, when their cars went into the shop for service. With a fleet of seventeen cars, Jack was now in the rental business, almost by default.

By 2008, Enterprise's fleet of rental cars had grown ever so slightly, to just under a million.

However, leasing was still king when I climbed on board twelve years after that seventeen car beginning in '62. Daily rental was considered by many to be merely a "way-station" for those privileged few who would some day enter the vaunted ranks of the almighty leasing department.

I definitely noticed the mind set of those in the leasing ranks, with their air of superiority and swaggering cocksure attitude. They were the golden children; the lily white prima donnas who sat in their offices, puffing on their pipes, reading the Wall Street Journal, and looking with disdain at the poor rental people working their asses off. At the end of the business day, they were the ones who waltzed over to the rental counter, and held their manicured hand out for a set of car keys to get them home. If a car happened to be low on fuel they'd groan if they had to stop at a filling station to put in enough gasoline to get them to and from their lovely domiciles in the posh suburbs.

If you were good looking and from a well connected wealthy family, your stay in the lowly rental department might well be limited to just a few weeks. With the right connections, a cushy leasing job could easily be arranged in a short period of time. I used to get frustrated when I was a young branch rental manager, and get tossed some lazy rich boy to bide his time until he could slide into that glamour position with some of his other cronies from their prep school days.

Some of the rich boys actually had a good work ethic, and I tried to convince them to stay in the rental department, to no avail. They had been pre-sold on the concept that leasing was the easiest, most lucrative and certainly the most beneficial path for their careers; so off they would go, and I'd get another rookie to train, not really knowing if they were going to stay in rental, or head for the ivory tower.

Usually, if they came in with the notion that the rental experience was only going to be temporary, their attitude reflected that. I wanted to fire one rich lazy son of a bitch who was rude to customers and never got up to write a rental agreement to save his life. I was told to forget it; this guy was going into leasing soon, so just deal with it.

This guy knew he was immune from any repercussion, so he used to thrive on being blatantly lazy. On one occasion when I was out of the office trying to drum up business from some local State Farm agents, a customer walked in the office to rent a car. Old Lazy Boy, who had a wide selection of cars to rent, told the customer there must be some mistake; there was no reservation for anybody with that name. After doing much exhaustive research, the laziest man in Enterprise history discovers that the reservation was inadvertently made at the Clayton office.

Big deal; the customer was standing right in front of him, credit card in hand and should have gotten a car right then and there. That would have required too much effort from our future leasing superstar; he made this poor gentleman grab a ride with his friend over to the Clayton branch, where a giggling Dave Dieckmann, Clayton's rental manager, got him going.

That night happened to be "softball night" and Dave could hardly contain himself telling me what happened earlier in the day, knowing full well that my lazy temporary trainee would never mention it to me. With Dave's broad face grinning like a Cheshire cat after gleefully giving me the play by play of what went on that day, I turned to our young stud shortstop who overheard Dave's very loud recollection, and before I could even begin, he just said "Big deal", and turned away.

That night, playing third base, I made a nice play on a slow roller, ranging far to my left, gloving the ball in front of this asshole, doing a complete 360, and firing a strike to first base to nab the runner. I somehow felt better about losing the deal now. I never even looked at Lazy Boy as I ambled back to my position at third base, although he was babbling something to the effect, "Yeah, take it in; nice play; take it in."

Then there were the solid, hard working rental guys who resented the system so much, they left the company altogether. Their principles got in the way of practicality. I saw their philosophical point, but I also had hope for the future, that the scales would start tipping in the direction of the rental side. Making matters worse, the rental managers were experiencing very tough times, financially, in the early '80s. Thanks to high interest rates, resulting in vey high costs, we were struggling to make any kind of profit; and without profit, we didn't make commissions.

I'd listen to the gloating lease salesmen coming over to talk to some of the rental people, in an effort to recruit them; saying things like,

"You're too good to be wasting your time in rental", or "Hope you're having fun washing those cars". Somewhere along the line, some imaginative leasing asshole, coined the expression, "daily reptile" when referring to a rental car. I must admit, I thought that was pretty funny.

Aside from inventing funny names for "daily rental", many of these assholes knew little or nothing about the business, but that didn't stop them from being the boss of the whole branch.

A classic example of ineptitude came back in my South Kingshighway days when our fearless leasing leader, Larry Snow, reprimanded Ed about not having enough rental personnel available to handle all the incoming phone calls. His solution: "From now on, you will not give rides to customers. Tell them they need to find their own way in and their own way back. We can't leave these phones unattended!"

Naturally, we had to ignore those orders and sneak in and out to give rides to customers. We pretty much got away with it, because the genius was holed up in his office with the blinds drawn most of the time, happily doing nothing at all.

We had no national advertising in those days, but if we did, with this mutant Larry's way of doing business, we might have been known as "The Company that won't pick you up." That may have been just catchy enough to work. Perhaps this one works better: "Pick Enterprise. We won't pick you up." Here's an original one that I ran by a focus group on effective advertising in the car rental industry: "Need a ride? Go fuck yourself." Admittedly, that one may have been a little harsh. Here's a very nice polite one: "Thank you for not asking us for a ride. We're really too busy to be doing that."

It gets better. Early one winter morning, after a fairly heavy snowfall, Larry announces to everybody in the office, "We can't rent any cars today! It's too dangerous for anybody to be driving out there!" Nobody uttered a word, although everybody's mouth was now wide open. I hadn't seen that many jaws drop since Tiny Tim married

Miss Vicky on Johnny Carson's Tonight Show, or for that matter seeing that freak on Laugh In during his breakthrough ukulele strumming rendition of "Tiptoe Through the Tulips".

It was all I could do to act like I was intently listening to his absurdity without cracking up (In business, being able to do this is an absolute necessity if you want to be a long- term employee with practically any company). When he retreated back to the safety of his well-curtained office, I looked at a very beleaguered Ed, as he just stared straight ahead for a few seconds, in disbelief. Then he rolled his eyes like a teenager embarrassed by something stupid his father said in front of the kid's friends.

I burst out laughing, but Ed didn't think it was funny. He glumly looked down and wearily shook his head, very slowly, obviously contemplating how he was going to deal with this situation. It was barely after 8 am, and we had a lot of reservations to handle that day.

Wisely, Ed said, "Forget that shit. He'll be in his office all day, anyway." I chuckled my approval at that decision, and as the office collectively breathed a sigh of relief, we were back in business.

Ed was right; Snow stayed in his cozy office, just as snug as a bug in a rug, oblivious to all that danger going on, all day long. We must've rented close to thirty cars that day, which was a pretty fair amount for that branch, snow or no snow; although Snow didn't seem to know.

It was well after 6 pm when we wrapped things up for the day, and walked precariously out to our icy cars to head home. I shouted out to Ed, as he was firing up the Cutlass he randomly chose for his short trip home, "Be careful; it's dangerous out there!"

In the early '80s, when Enterprise opened the New Orleans market, they picked "Mr. Don't Drive Our Cars in the Snow" Snow to run the operation. Ironically, even though it rarely snows in New Orleans, Larry Snow was a total bust, and he was canned in short order. Of course, what was amazing to anybody who knew this hapless ninny was that he ever got promoted to begin with.

What got his foot inside the door was his leasing background and his desire to live in a place where snow is rarely seen; including that particular Snow, as he no doubt hid in his office most of the time in New Orleans.

Enterprise steadfastly clung to the notion that every city that opened would be powered by the profits from its leasing operation, which after all, was its primary business. The car rental business was still considered to be a lesser division of the company, because it got a five year later start than the leasing division. Gradually, as more new cities opened, the company realized the profits generated from rental came much quicker than the painstaking leasing process.

With the remarkable success of the rental department shaking the company's original business blue print to its very core, the change finally became acknowledged, and a company's philosophy regarding the management in the Groups throughout the company followed suit.

By the late '80s, Jack Taylor himself wondered out loud in a meeting with a handful of Officers (I happened to be one of them), "Why on earth are we still calling ourselves 'Enterprise Leasing' when we're more of a rental company?" When he looked in my direction after that rhetorical question, I just raised my eyebrows, in a whimsical, John Belushi-like way, and shrugged my shoulders; Jack knew.

By that time, I'd already had a firsthand experience of being rejected for a promotion to General Manager because I lacked the "necessary (leasing) credentials".

That was at the beginning of the decade. By the end of the decade, the mindset of the company had changed, even before Jack's official proclamation. Shortly after that meeting, the long-awaited announcement came down from the corporate hierarchy that Enterprise Leasing would have the name change operation, to Enterprise Rent-a-Car.

Soon, the national advertising campaign was launched, and cheesy Enterprise Rent-a-Car commercials were telecast on a national basis, and for some reason went in an entirely different direction than the strategy Larry Snow advocated. They were actually promoting the whole "pick up the customer" concept. I was shocked. Didn't they know how fucking inconvenient that was for us?

The car rental industry was about to be dominated by the company that started renting cars almost by accident, and survived some of its forgettable management decisions, such as ever hiring that other guy named Larry to begin with.

Years later, the entire leasing department was revamped, restructured, reorganized, and renamed. "Leasing" became "Fleet Services", and a couple of guys who would've been displaced by the reorganization were reassigned to other high-ranking corporate positions. I would eventually get tangled up in power struggles with both individuals, and for the first time in my career, feel the knife in my back.

Chapter 3

Remembering Andy Jansky

One of my favorite activities with Executive Leasing Company was the chance to mingle with the other employees in the St Louis Group every two or three months, while at the same time eating a great dinner.

Wayne Kaufmann and Doug Brown would typically lead the "dinner meeting" proceedings hammering home some sort of important issue that they wanted to make sure was clearly understood by everybody. Wayne was usually concerned about controlling costs and/or maximizing revenues, while Doug would go off on tangents about the upcoming car buys from the manufacturers or why rental guys couldn't become General Managers; or some other curious observation, which usually sailed over my head.

My biggest concern was usually, "Should I order the prime rib or the T-bone?"

During these gatherings, I got the chance to hang out with guys (Enterprise hadn't thought much of hiring women in those days, nor minorities for that matter) from other offices, including some of the topnotch rental managers around town that I viewed with awe, because some of those guys really knew how to sell; and my manager didn't.

As I gazed around the room at my very first dinner meeting in early '75, it struck me that this looked like some sort of Mormon convention; nothing but white guys in white shirts wearing nice conservative ties. That was the look that dominated the Enterprise landscape well into the '80s. Since the mid '90s, the company has taken a much more politically correct approach to recruiting, and the result has been a much more diverse workforce wearing those white shirts or blouses.

Clearly, in the mid '70s, the leaders seemed to be Don Marsh, who managed the North office, Dave Dieckmann who was in charge of the Clayton branch, and Andy Jansky, who managed the West County branch; an office I dreamed of working at, as I passed by it every morning on the way to South Kingshighway.

Jansky, my personal favorite, seemed to be the maverick in the Group; an outspoken, charismatic, and free-wheeling guy who had a magnetic personality, which exuded a smooth, confident, and whimsical charm. He seemed to feel at ease talking to anybody, including Kaufmann and Brown; both of whom scared the hell out of me, since they were the big bosses, and I was an insecure neophyte. I was perfectly happy staying invisible.

Jansky, on the other hand was so glib and charming as he handled every situation with such ease making everyone working for him always feel comfortable. I would tend to gravitate his way during these occasions, just to hear what funny stuff he had in his bag of tricks, and try to get to know him better, hoping that he'd like me enough to not object, if I were to ever be transferred to his office.

Gradually, as another dinner meeting was winding down, Doug Brown was sitting at a table with a half dozen or so rental people and talking that rapid-fire chain-smoking raspy banter he was known for; as I recall he was explaining something about an upcoming car buy.

Jansky was grousing a bit as he looked in Doug's direction, because as Andy saw it, Doug was one of those "leasing assholes" who supported the philosophy that only the leasing people were smart enough to become General Managers; a concept that rankled Andy, who as a college kid working his way through St Louis University, started with the company by washing cars, and then gradually worked his way into the office, where he learned the rental business from the ground floor up.

Andy was a true "rental guy" and he would never even consider switching teams to head to the leasing side; in fact, if anybody went from rental to leasing, they were automatically considered a traitor, by the head of the rental army, Andy Jansky.

I think the subject only came up once or twice, since I had the same sentiment, but when Andy would tell me, "Larry, don't go into leasing. They're all a bunch of assholes;" I tended to agree, as I tried to think of someone from that department who might not be classified as an asshole, to no avail. I had no desire, whatsoever, to head over to that side of the business, although I was never really positive Executive Leasing would ever change its mindset; actually, I never really worried about it that much, unlike my pal Andy, who was still fuming as he glared at the guy he referred to as "the Brown man".

The first time I ever talked to Andy on the phone, was shortly after the first time I ever met him, at my first dinner meeting; he thought he'd run one of his comedy routines by me one day when he called the office and I answered.

In a cartoonish voice that had distinct Mel Blanc characteristics, Andy inquired, "Is this the Mortician?" Andy had a way of elongating the last word in a sentence, which I found to be hilarious, although on this particular occasion, I wasn't really sure who the crazy person on the other end was. I was amused, and had an idea it was Andy, but I needed to continue the comedy routine, to get a positive ID on the culprit; saying, "Mortician?" Then he said, "Undertaker!"

Realizing this indeed the inimitable Andy Jansky, I got the joke, which was a new one on me: Underwood sounded like Undertaker, which of course meant that I was surely the Mortician. He seemed delighted that I went along with his gag; then cheerfully asked to talk to Ed. I thought to myself, "Eh, what's up, Doc?" I knew this would be a good guy to work with, since we both seemed to think life was too important to take it seriously.

Right around my one-year anniversary with the company, I was still plugging along as "the number three guy" at the same old office. Ed's assistant, an amusing but somewhat self absorbed guy I'll call "Bruce", who would've made a terrific Elvis impersonator, had expressed an interest in an opening in Orlando; this would've been only a lateral move, but for Bruce, the idea of getting out of St Louis and heading to the consistently beautiful climate of north-central Florida sounded much more enticing than what he now had.

Lanny Dakus, the gregarious pioneer of the Florida operation, who years later opened the Big Apple, the New York Group, in the late '80s, was genuinely enthused about anything to do with the rental business, had the gift of gab to get the results he needed to excel; and in the end, had a very successful career.

On this particular early autumn day in 1975, Lanny flies up to St Louis just to interview Bruce, so it was apparent, the chances of getting Bruce out of there were pretty good.

Bruce suddenly realized he was lacking in the wardrobe department, as the only suit he owned now looked like shit after well over a year in the rental trenches, so he wisely decided to invest in one to make a favorable impression with Lanny.

Bruce and his mutton chop sideburns proceeded to head down to the nearby JC Penney where he grabbed a suit off the rack, thought it fit great (it was too big), and wore it back to the office, tags and all. He was so busy admiring himself; he forgot to take the tags off his stylish electric blue suit. Soon, Lanny arrives with all the furor of a tornado and sweeps Bruce away for about an hour in the back office we used as a lunchroom, to conduct the big interview.

Afterwards, I asked Bruce how things went. Dramatically, he slowly turns to me with those little tags still bobbing around, takes a drag from his cigarette, and says with a straight face, "Lanny told me, 'Bruce, I like you. I like you a lot.'" At the end of the sentence, a cloud of white smoke masks his face and tags, as he eases into his favorite chair; quite satisfied with himself.

Bruce got the job. Then I got his old job without even having to interview for it or make a wardrobe change. By this time, Ed kind of liked me.

Andy Jansky was one of the first people outside of my office to congratulate me on moving up. He lived maybe a quarter mile away, on Itaksa, so he'd pop in from time to time, unexpectedly.

The subject quickly shifted to a discussion Bruce had with Andy right after Bruce got the Orlando gig. Andy, who was the master of lampooning people who took themselves too seriously, told me that he and Bruce had a "heart to heart talk" about the future, and what it might hold in store for both.

Naturally, Bruce initiated the conversation, which Andy hilariously imitated for me. Andy was now Bruce, and I was now Andy for this particular reenactment. Andy got right in my face, put his right hand on my left shoulder, paused, gave me the perfect Bruce blank expression, and said, "Andy, what are your goals?" The last word of the sentence lasted about five seconds. Just to make sure I heard it right, he repeated it again, with even greater emphasis on the word "goals".

I cracked up. This was classic Jansky sarcasm, and it was right on the money. Bruce was so serious about everything it just had to be funny, at least to Andy and his up and coming protégé, me.

A few months later, after another dinner meeting, Andy was fuming about Don Marsh getting the promotion to become the first City Manager in St Louis Group history; at the time, this new position was created to give Kaufmann more time to spend on the company's ever growing rental business, as a whole; Jansky felt he deserved the promotion, but got aced out by a guy who had an overall good reputation and seemed to be the more stable of the two; Jansky seemed a bit too zany and irreverent, in retrospect, and had a history of doing some pretty flakey deals; in other words, renting cars to deadbeats and getting burned a lot.

Charisma lost over consistency. Don did a pretty good job, as far as I could tell, but Andy never seemed to warm up to Marsh, whom Andy referred to as "Marshmallow".

About six months after I became the assistant manager of the South Kingshighway office, Kaufmann and Marshmallow decide to shake things up, by sending me to West County. In return, West County's assistant, Terry O'Connell, got shipped over to my old office. Naturally, I'm delighted to make the move, but I'm not so sure Terry felt the same way.

One person who definitely didn't want to see Terry leave was the branch secretary, Jo Ann Kindle. Jo Ann was married to the manager of the Midtown office, a stoic country boy named Bob Kindle.

She also happened to be the daughter of Jack C Taylor, the great entrepreneur who founded Enterprise back in '57. Jo Ann, of course, had a brother, Andy, who would later ace out Doug Brown for President of the company. However, Jo Ann didn't act like she had anything special going for her, except her ability to do great office work, and be friends with the guys in the office.

She liked Terry and didn't want to see him go. She didn't know me, and was a little standoffish at first. I could understand that; in fact, she let me know her feelings right away, so I tried to be as charming as possible so I'd eventually get her stamp of approval.

Actually, we hit it off right away. In fact, the entire office was like one big happy family. I loved working there and really had a blast every day with Andy's antics keeping us all amused. Andy seemed to enjoy the role of being the company maverick, and seemed to thrive on taking a chance on just about anybody who wanted to rent a car. It was almost like he was challenging anybody to burn him; and from time to time, they did; but it always seemed Andy would come out smelling like a rose in the long run.

Back in West County's service department, Andy had a hilarious sidekick, a hulking, wisecracking, country-bred, and lovable bear of a man known as Harry Boyd. Harry was to Andy Jansky as Andy Devine's "Jingles" was to Wild Bill Hickock; the perfect compliment to a daring cowboy; Harry used to mimic Andy's disdain for the system, even before the system really became a system; but then it was the innocent loathing of a guy I really kind of liked; none other than Jansky's leasing nemesis, Doug Brown. Harry would brag about something or other and how that would surely get under the skin of "the Brown man" while I just smiled and nodded my approval.

Promptly at 6 pm, Harry would religiously pop the tab from a nice cold refreshing, Falstaff Beer, a swill that at first seemed so horrible I couldn't believe people actually bought it. Strangely enough, after a few months, this beer started tasting good, as if I had been brought under some weird hypnotic spell, but after a long day in the trenches, it seemed like the perfect elixir; the brew Harry affectionately called "golden cold ones".

Adding to Harry's lovable charm was the fact that he was a beekeeper, on the side; every now and then, some desperate housewife would call up the office, terrified about a nest of bees that had relocated to her attic, and Jo Ann would page Harry, "Harry Bee; phone call on line one. Harry Bee; line one." Off Harry would go, dressed in his aviary outfit to keep him safe from possible bee stings, collect the nest, and gently relocate it somewhere out in the safety and serenity of the nearby woods.

Harry Boyd was cool and truly a jack of all trades; he was also the West County designated barbeque chef, making the best ribs imaginable for a hungry lunch time bunch; I was usually the gopher, heading down to the local Schnuck's grocery store a couple of miles east on Manchester Road to buy whatever it was Harry would cook up; generally speaking, practically any day without rain was a good day for a little West County BBQ.

Together, the Andy and Harry show was a big hit at the fun-loving West County office, and Jo Ann was the executive producer. Of course, she was in awe of the star of the show, Andy Jansky, and so was everyone else in the branch.

Jo Ann once told me, "Andy's the luckiest guy who ever lived. He once had a car stolen from him while he was making sales calls in East St Louis. Andy somehow managed to track it down within an hour, and stole it right back!" Jo Ann's eyes were wide open with amazement and amusement, at the conclusion of that tale, as I'm sure mine were also. But she was right; it seemed as though Andy could do no wrong.

Soon after my arrival at the rollicking West County traveling circus, Andy gives me the first of several nicknames I'd garner during my career: "Lawrence of Arabia", but with Andy's version, the last syllable in "Arabia" goes on for about five seconds, until the "ah" just fades away. It was hysterical; the whole office got a kick out of it, and of course everybody started calling me that now. After a while, Andy shortened it to "Arabia" although the rest of the office either stuck with the whole nickname, or called me "Lawrence". By this time, practically nobody called me "Larry", and that was fine by me; who wanted to be named after one of the Three Stooges, anyway; especially the least popular one?

Jansky's most celebrated nickname within the ranks of Enterprise was for the "collision damage waiver" car rental companies try its best to sell to their customers; "CDW" was too cumbersome for Andy, so he came up with "dub" (the beginning of pronouncing "W"); and more than likely, that expression is still being used today out there in Enterprise land.

Shortly after America celebrates its bicentennial, the West County office has some fireworks of its own causing quite a stir. Andy rents a car to some guy who was staying in a nearby fleabag motel. The guy didn't have a credit card so Andy rolls the car (of course, he sold the "dub") with a small cash deposit. The guy was supposed to have the car only for the day but he disappears. The front desk clerk of the motel tells Andy he split, owing them some money.

I was oblivious to the problem until I saw Andy's ashen face. Holding the rental contract in his left hand while swatting it with his right hand, he said, "Fuck, this asshole stole the goddamn car!" I'd never seen Andy worried about a rental going bad before, but this time he knew it was really bad. I tried to sound optimistic saying something like maybe he decided to keep it for just another day. Andy just shook his head and said, "Arabia, he even stole the goddamn pillows from the motel!"

In other words, this guy was long gone; and now would be living in the car until the police find him; and that could take months, years, or never happen at all.

If ever there was a deal that never should've been done, this was it, and Andy knew it. A couple of days after the deal's declared very bad, and reported to the police as a stolen car, a very pissed off Andy Taylor pops into the office to have a few words with Jansky. Taylor would later become the head-honcho for the entire corporation, but on this particular summer afternoon, he's quite displeased about a Chevrolet Caprice that has been practically given away.

During the brief course of the closed door reaming, I look over to Jo Ann and ask her if she thinks her brother is going to fire Andy. She just says, "No, but he's in a whole lot of trouble." Jo Ann just rolls her eyes while making that assessment, and I could see this was no laughing matter, at all.

The mood was unusually somber in the office for the next week or so, as the car was still unaccounted for, and feared gone forever. Jansky hardly said a word and I kept my mouth shut too, because I knew there was really nothing to be said. It was a bad deal; and nothing could change that fact.

Then one day, the police called to report the car had been recovered, undamaged, in Memphis. The guy was apparently driving the car very slowly, following some young ladies, who were walking down Beale Street. A police officer became suspicious of this activity, and pulled the creep over. After running a check on the plates and discovering that this was a stolen car, we got it back in one piece, pillows and all. Andy had lucked out again. Jo Ann just looked at me and said, "See?" Her eyes were wide open in amazement, again.

Back in the service department, a gleeful Harry Boyd just grinned and said, "Lassie came home!" Over the years, any car that was missing in action, Harry would call "Lassie", hoping that she'd somehow find her way home. Naturally, when this particular "Lassie" came home, it was time to celebrate; Harry cooked up some wonderful ribs, and all was well again at West County.

A few weeks later, Andy quietly pulls me aside to tell me he's going to be opening a new branch in South County. This comes as quite a surprise to me and I ask him why he'd leave the West County gold mine to start up a brand new office from scratch. He just said, "Arabia, I'm bored here. I need to do something different. Besides, I'm going to make sure you get this office. You deserve it." A few weeks later, he was gone and I was the new manager of the branch that he built into a consistent cash cow; and I still never even had to interview to get promoted.

After Andy opened his doors for business, I'd go down to visit from time to time. The place was literally a hole in the wall, right next door to a pizza joint near Tesson Ferry and Gravois. I must admit, the office smelled great, but it didn't have air conditioning and there wasn't room for more than three people to squeeze in there. Andy's assistant was the good-natured Stan Mann, who would eventually help open Dallas in the late '70s, spend the big '80s working at corporate, and then open Boston in the early '90s, before retiring in 2002.

Andy and Stan built the fleet of that little hole in the wall branch up past 100 cars in no time at all (which seemed like a significant milestone for any office), and about a year later, Andy was promoted to a City Manager's position in Houston. He needed something big, and this was it. When Andy took over the Houston Group's rental department, it was really struggling to say the least, but not for long.

Within a few months, his magic produced an operation that consistently outperformed the rest of the other Groups in the company. Soon, if you wanted to lead the company in any measurable category, you'd have to surpass Houston to do so; trying to chase down my old pal was really kind of fun; on the rare occasions my branch posted numbers better than the Houston Group average, Andy was always quick to send me a little congratulatory note, through the inter-company e-mail; usually something simple like; "Way to go, Arabia." Then he'd throw in a little wisecrack, like; "Don't go thinking that'll ever happen again."

Andy's charismatic leadership was incredibly successful. He proved that having fun, while maintaining good customer and employee relations, created the right environment to breed success.

As his career was rocketing upward at a remarkable pace, with seemingly no end in sight, tragically, in May of 1982, Andy Jansky's life was cut short in a car accident.

By then, I was working in Phoenix as the City Manager. Jo Ann Kindle tearfully called one Saturday morning to tell me the bad news. Anyone who knew Andy Jansky went to that funeral on an appropriately rainy day in South St Louis.

During the funeral service, crying unabashedly, I remember thinking I just lost my best friend. As I looked at the grief stricken faces of the other people cramped inside that tiny Catholic diocese with me, I knew they all felt the same way.

Chapter 4
"Tell Us Another Story, Uncle Larry!"

Anybody who knows me well knows I like to tell stories. If the subject matter is baseball, I could go on for hours; actually, I have gone on for hours; I'm a regular baseball historian.

Thanks in large part to growing up in St Louis, where baseball is revered and understood far more than any simple "pastime"; St Louis fans are widely regarded as the most knowledgeable in all of baseball.

To a typical St Louis Cardinals fan, baseball represents the essence of joy or sorrow, every single day of any given season, depending on the outcome of any game, whether played in April or September; if the Cardinals were still mathematically in the hunt for post season play, that was good enough for me to maintain my optimism with every victory or cringe over any heartbreaking loss.

As a franchise, the Cardinals have been successful in winning World Championships more than any other National League team, and rank second in all of baseball, with ten titles. The New York Yankees are in the number one position, with 1,592 World Series Championships, as everyone knows; but they would've had 1,593 titles, had the Cardinals not beaten them, mercilessly, in the 1964 World Series (actually, the damned Yankees have won something like 26 World Championships). How about that?

One day during my tenure as rental manager of the West County office, I was giving my employees a little dose of baseball history, telling the story about a turn of the century ballplayer known as "Dummy" Hoy. I was always fascinated with the old nicknames given to the ballplayers in the early days.

It didn't matter that customers were everywhere, demanding to be waited on, like they were important. What mattered to me was that baseball players had funny nicknames, sometimes; and these stories had to be told to my people.

Everybody knows about "Babe" Ruth, who was also known as the "Sultan of Swat" and the "Bambino". I'm not sure why "Sultan of Syphilis" never caught on; or "Bam-Bang-Bimbo", but he was after all, the great American hero and there was some sort of image to promulgate. Yeah, that movie made in the '40s, starring William Bendix as the Bambino, was pretty much total bullshit; but of course, I cried like a baby the first time I saw it. Come to think of it, the one with John Goodman, another local St Louis boy (South County) about my age, was even worse, although slightly more accurate. That one just made me cringe; Goodman's acting was good, but the script sucked.

Perhaps the ultimate American hero, a man immortalized by Hemmingway, and Simon and Garfunkel alike; was "Joltin' Joe" DiMaggio; the "Yankee Clipper", who seemed to glide through life, effortlessly performing his tasks on and off the baseball field, with such aplomb, he almost seemed bored by it all. He was the epitome of cool, The Great DiMaggio.

DiMaggio was even cool when he decided to retire from the game he once performed with such effortless superiority; physical limitations now prevented him from being that type of player and he knew it; so he quit, and that was all there was to it. It seems some kid by the name of Mantle was ready to emerge as the next great Yankee.

The cool DiMaggio naturally married the hottest woman on the planet, Marilyn Monroe. However, proving that not everything can be perfect between two seemingly perfect people, they quickly divorced. There must've been at least one wise guy who now labeled him "Jilted Joe" DiMaggio.

Then there was Frank "Home Run" Baker who led the American League in home runs for four consecutive years with the grand total of 39 home runs during that time. Back in the "dead ball era", that seemed like a prodigious total; hence the nickname. Nowadays, averaging about ten home runs a year would probably give Frank the nickname "Frances".

Nicknames given to baseball players weren't always flattering, as they quite often pointed out a physical characteristic or worse, a deformity the poor player may have possessed; and no one seemed to care whether or not the accompanying nickname hurt his little feelings or not. There's no sniveling in baseball.

Take for example, the case of one Mordecai "Three Finger" Brown; erstwhile pitcher during baseball's pre-Sultan of Swat dead ball era, who had a Hall of Fame career with that uniquely deformed three fingered pitching hand.

If he was offended by the nickname, he certainly never manifested any such emotions in public.

First of all, with a name like "Mordecai" almost anything else would be an improvement. Secondly, any sign of emotional distress on his part, surely would've been mercilessly attacked by opponents with such ferocity, that an addendum to the original nickname would probably be tacked on, for good measure. "Three Finger" Brown may have evolved into "Three Finger Cry Baby" Brown; or even more sarcastic, "Where's Your Other Finger?" Brown. Wisely, I think, Mordecai left well enough alone, and became the best three-fingered pitcher the game has known.

One of my favorite pieces of baseball folklore was the story of a deaf mute named William Ellsworth Hoy (the story I alluded to earlier in this diatribe) who bounced around several teams in the late 19th century and early 20th century. Early in his career, some asshole started calling him "Dummy", and the next thing you knew, everybody was calling him that. Nobody seemed to care if poor William took offense to the nickname, almost as if to say, "He can't hear, so what difference does it make? Isn't that right, Dummy? See, he doesn't seem to mind at all."

Dummy was a speedy centerfielder and on fly balls hit anywhere in his direction, his teammates knew to get out of his way whenever they heard the loud, high pitched squeal (almost like an ambulance letting other vehicles know to get out of the way) coming from his throat that told them, "I've got it! Dummy is in the house! Hoop, here I am!" Silence from the non-ventriloquist Dummy meant he felt reaching that ball in time to prevent it from landing safely on the ground was as likely as him hearing the National Anthem being played before the umpires would silently (from Dummy's perspective) lip sync "Play ball!" Actually, that whole National Anthem thing started after Dummy's time, but it made for a reasonable analogy.

In addition, to avoid any possible confusion on his part about the outcome of a particular play, the umpires got together and had a focus group meeting on "How to Deal with the Issues of the Deaf Mute in Baseball", and after a number of committee meetings, a few lunches back and forth, and a couple of conference calls, they somehow got together and began motioning the result by using their arms and hands in the manner that is still used today.

The "safe" call, with both arms fully extended, with palms down, almost looks like the umpire is trying to fly, or perhaps glide serenely through the air. On close plays, the umpire had to "sell" the result to the team coming out on the short end of the stick. Indecisiveness was intolerable, but of course, emphatic incompetence was even worse. No matter how decisive the umpire signaled the play, if replays showed he screwed up, the whole baseball world knew.

Just ask Don Denkinger, the beleaguered umpire who blew the call at first base in the 1985 World Series, when St Louis was just three outs away from the championship. Replays showed how badly he missed that call; by about three feet or so; but perhaps in the heat of the moment, feeling the pressure to be decisive, he may have panicked, and made the "safe" call instead of the correct "out" call.

If Don had a few extra seconds to think about it, take his time, and ponder the actual outcome of what really happened; with the runner arriving at the bag just a little late, he might have casually told the world, "Well, guys; after taking a quick peek at the replay, just to make sure I get this right, it looks like he was about as out as he could be", and that would have been that; the smiling Cardinals probably would have gone on to win the game, and of course, the Series; and Don would not have been regarded as some big dummy, especially in St Louis.

A young trainee by the name of Steve Merrick, who always seemed fascinated by my monologues, but apparently not particularly fascinated with work, decided to give me the infamous nickname, in the summer of '78, which would stick for the duration of my career, when he blurted out, "Tell us another story, Uncle Larry!"

Steve really liked that Dummy Hoy story, and thanks to his spontaneous outburst, now it seemed everybody really liked calling me "Uncle Larry". Steve went on to leave the company shortly after tagging me with the fucking nickname that would refuse to leave. Rumors that he actually got sick and tired of listening to my bullshit and had to get away were completely unfounded, as far as I could tell.

Having a last name like Underwood, and growing up to derisive taunts such as, "Underwear" or "Underdog", I never objected to my new, improved nickname and I never thought it would be an issue with even the biggest asshole in the Enterprise corporate hierarchy. After all, it was Uncle Larry who got promoted to the City Manager position in Phoenix, and it was Uncle Larry who became the General Manager of the newly formed West Group, just five years later.

It seemed to me, the whole "Uncle Larry" persona was a harmless diversion, and after a while, it seemed to work in favor of helping reduce the terror level a young trainee may have felt when meeting the big shot General Manager for the first time. It would not be uncommon for a brand new employee, who has never met me to walk right up to me, introduce themselves to "Uncle Larry" the terror-free General Manager and start talking to me as though they've known me for their entire lives.

Generally speaking, putting "Uncle" in front of somebody's name seems to automatically turn that person into someone less intimidating, maybe a little goofy, but lovable and good natured; and I saw no harm in that. Over the years, there have been many notable "Uncle's" in stage, screen, television, and music to that support that notion:

Buck (John Candy's lovable buffoon), Fester (made bald heads cool for a while), Joe (moving kind of slow at the junction), Albert (we're so sorry), Billy (dimwitted but lovable; almost caused his nephew, George to commit suicide), Ben (famous for white rice), Charlie (always yelling at Robbie, Chip and Ernie), Cracker (cool musician, flowing like a fish in the sea), Milton (the cross dressing comedian of early television), and Sam (America's role model ever since World War II, who wants you, of all people).

During my stint with the Phoenix Group I put together a regular newsletter entitled, "Uncle Larry's Roadrunner Report", and that first issue was especially hilarious. The word I received back from corporate was that Don Ross, one of the head-honchos, could be heard laughing his ass off in his office while reading my comedic prose. I liked Don; he always had a good sense of humor.

A couple of years later, when I was the General Manager of the newly formed West Group, I put together another newsletter; this time cleverly entitled, "Uncle Larry's Wild, Wild West". I thought it was pretty good, too. I even had a little column I'd dole out every month, called "Uncle Larry sez". As far as I knew, nobody at corporate was going around saying, "What in the hell has gotten into

Underwood? What's with this 'Uncle Larry' bullshit? What an asshole!"

It wasn't until early 2000, when I got a heartwarming memo from my corporate ass-clown that this nickname suddenly became such a controversial issue. According to the hierarchy, I was now regarded as someone who could not possibly be considered a well-respected General Manager while allowing any of the employees to call me "Uncle Larry".

That's the kind of bullshit that indicates the recipient's career is heading south, so I addressed the matter in what I felt to be the most appropriate manner when I replied to my corporate tormentor in a written memo, very formally, "I'm now the artist formerly known as Uncle Larry".

With that issue firmly addressed, I supposed I should've also sent out the following memo to all West Group employees, but it slipped my mind:

"It is now against company policy to refer to me as 'Uncle Larry'. I'm trying to get some respect here, people, okay? Any violation of this very serious newly created policy will be dealt with in a very serious manner, seriously; I hope this doesn't upset you; this doesn't mean I don't love you; I do love you; I'm just not in love with you."

Lawrence A Underwood
Vice President/General Manager

Chapter 5
My Blueprint For Success

Much has already been written about the man who had the foresight to launch his new car leasing company, called Executive Leasing, in 1957. Jack C Taylor is one of the greatest entrepreneurs in American business history, building an empire by putting customer service above everything else. His management style, which gave autonomy to the people under him, proved successful because those people, for the most part, followed Jack's original business blueprint quite well; and when they didn't, they were replaced.

Nowadays, every management trainee in the company understands the formula for success, which helps explain why Enterprise is so big and profitable; but there's more to it than taking care of every customer's whim. What has pushed Enterprise over the top, to the point where they're generally speaking, year in and year out, making more profit than all the other rental companies, combined; is their uncanny ability to squeeze every last dollar out of every rental transaction.

The managers that could get every employee in the branch to understand that concept, and put it into action, were the ones most likely to succeed in the long haul. I took pride in my ability to generate strong revenue because I had a passion for selling and I made sure everybody in the office put every ounce of energy they had into getting the most out of every transaction as possible. We used to call it "selling up", an expression first coined by the original head-honcho of daily rental, Wayne Kaufmann.

With the income and expense per unit analysis that came out on a monthly basis (the original Enterprise "measuring stick"), there was no hiding a poor performing branch. Woe to any manager who would be on the bottom of that list; I'd been there a few times, and it sucked; but more often than not, I was at or near the top of the heap.

Wayne probably had the most impact of how I'd conduct business than anybody else in the company. When he was preaching the importance of maximizing revenue while minimizing expenses, I relentlessly pursued every dollar I could get from the customer, while scrutinizing every dime that was being spent. I became known as the biggest tightwad in town, but to me that was a badge of honor, simply the best way to run a business.

Wayne always said the rental business is really very simple; it seemed those people who were always trying to reinvent the wheel were really only spinning their wheels. Wayne, in his rural Missouri drawl, always spoke deliberately, in a Jimmy Stewart-like understated fashion.

As far as selling was concerned, he'd simply say, "You've got to practice, practice, practice." Then he'd say the most effective way to run the business is using the "K.I.S.S" approach: "Keep it simple, stupid." That always seemed like the smart approach to me; after all, it was only natural for me to keep things simple, because I'm fairly simple minded; and looking back on it, I'm glad I am simple minded; I would be the poster child for the K.I.S.S. approach, for sure.

Wayne was certainly no dummy; his simple approach to the business got him to the top of the company ladder, making him the first Officer to rise through the ranks of the once lowly rental department. His promotion to "Vice President of Daily Rental" was announced at a companywide rental manager's meeting, in 1980, which brought one of the loudest and longest ovations I can ever recall at any company function; thinking about it still brings tears to my eyes; and that's a fact.

Guys who had paid their dues for a lot longer than me, and were getting frustrated with the company's leasing over rental mentality were really cheering the loudest and longest; guys like Andy Jansky, who had already proved the good things he could do in Houston, and who was getting restless to join Wayne in the ranks of the Officers, bred strictly in rental.

I had just made a lateral move, taking over the prestigious Clayton office, just days ahead of this particular meeting, and I was somewhat embarrassed to have managers from outside of St Louis coming up to me and congratulating me for the move. I remember telling one of my St Louis cohorts, Gail Anderson, one of the very first females to make it all the way to a branch rental manager's position, "I don't get it. All I did was move from one office to another; big deal."

As it would play out, inside of a year, that simple lateral move helped set the stage for something quite big for me, which really guided my career in an unbelievably positive direction, for its twenty-six year duration. Again, the simplicity of what had just taken place seemed to be the catalyst for my future success.

Doug Brown, the guy with the leasing background, but also had a great understanding of what it took to be successful in rental; always said, "You've got to do the basic blocking and tackling if you're going to make it work."

Doug sounded like Vince Lombardi, legendary coach of the Green Bay Packers, when talking in such simple terms; but like Lombardi, who wouldn't tolerate sloppy fundamentals, Brown got his point across to anyone interested in making Enterprise a long-term and successful career; I listened to every word he said, and tried to incorporate his philosophy, along with Wayne's, into how I would go about my business of first running a branch, then a department, and eventually, an entire Group, with multiple departments.

Doug and Wayne didn't always agree on certain issues, but their fundamental business philosophies were very similar. Whatever they were doing seemed to work, so I tried to pattern myself as much as possible to both guys; they were, along with Jack Taylor and Andy Jansky, my original role models.

Wayne and Doug both left the company around the same time; in the early '90s; and I don't think it was much of a coincidence that Enterprise started acting like a big bureaucracy shortly thereafter; and as practically everybody knows, big bureaucracies don't like anything simple, which is an unfortunate, but all too recurring state of affairs in most large corporations.

I think the obvious reason why corporate bureaucracies become such complex and micro-managing entities is based on one simple motivating factor: Fear.

Big corporations are especially in this litigious day and age, extremely afraid of lawsuits; the slightest impropriety from anywhere within their massive empires, whether it be from a sexual harassment claim, wrongful termination claim, miscellaneous negligence claim, or any of the other assorted discrimination claims that always seem to pop up; causes a trickle down effect to its now paranoid corporate officers or managers in the field.

The fear that the big corporation has in its attempt to avoid trouble, now becomes the catalyst for the fear that all their nervous mid-level to high-level managers have, trying to placate their immediate supervisors, to maintain the safe status-quo.

"Fear" then becomes the root cause of the inevitable backstabbing so prevalent nowadays, especially in big business; as the frightened drones try to present themselves in a favorable light to their now intimidating bosses, in the process, quite often decide the best way to protect themselves is by causing the downfall of others. With others now looking incompetent, the backstabber appears to be quite competent, and deemed worthy for continued employment, at least for the time being.

It's really very simple; and for a person like myself, who hates that mentality, all I can say is, "Kiss off."

The only difference of opinion I had with Doug was the same thing guys like Andy Jansky despised; and that was the leasing over rental mentality, which kept some of its best talent on the sidelines while allowing some of its worst talent to rear its ugly head.

As luck would have it, I'd be right in the middle of such a controversy, even after receiving a huge promotion that would take me out of St Louis to the Arizona desert, in the spring of 1981. About a year after that, all hell would break loose during a meeting, and the company would never be the same again, although I would still be the same old simple-minded Uncle Larry.

Chapter 6
Jack's Son Andy

I don't remember the first time I met Jack Taylor's son, Andy. In fact, I don't even remember when I heard that Jack had a son named Andy, and that Andy happened to work at Executive Leasing, too. That information gradually filtered down to me in the trenches, and really had no consequence to me; I still had to wash those cars, write up those rental contracts, and occasionally deal with somewhat difficult customers, while putting in my usual 50 to 60 hour work-week.

Quite possibly, the first time I heard that "Andy Taylor" worked for Executive Leasing, I wondered if Barney Fife had a job in accounting, or if Goober Pyle worked in the Clayton service department.

There may have been some Barneys, Goobers, or even Floyds working for the company, but I didn't know them; and as far as I was concerned, the fact that Jack's son Andy worked for the company was neither surprising nor controversial; if any employees thought Taylor family nepotism caused sonny boy to unfairly land a nice job with Executive Leasing, I was oblivious to it.

The notoriously outspoken Andy Jansky never groused about Andy

Taylor's position in the company, nor Doug Brown's for that matter; the only thing that got under Jansky's skin was the his general resentment about the leasing over rental syndrome, which Jack's son nor Doug could really do much to change; even though they probably never thought it was worth changing anyway.

I always thought the two guys I interviewed with, Doug Brown and Wayne Kaufmann were the top dogs in the company, after Andy's dad, Jack; at least that was the perception I had. Somewhere around the end of the '70s, Andy emerged as the official President of the Company, over Doug Brown, a move that perplexed more than a few people inside the company.

The inside scoop I got from Andy Taylor's brother-in-law, Bob Kindle (Midtown's branch rental manager who transferred to the non-automotive division of the company) was that Doug slightly tarnished his credibility when a non-automotive business deal he put together went astray; whether or not that had anything to do with Doug getting passed over for the Presidency is pure conjecture; but it now seemed unlikely the Brown man would ever become the head-honcho of the company Jack built.

Before that power play took place, the Andy Taylor I eventually came to know ran the St Louis Group, although I rarely had any direct contact with him myself; until I got promoted to branch rental manager of the West County office, in September of 1976.

Before I took over the reigns of that office, Andy wanted to have a few words with me, to make sure I had my head screwed on properly. Not knowing what else to do, I pretended to have my head screwed on properly as I met with him for the first time ever, in his humble little office (in those days, everybody's office was humble) next door to the Clayton branch.

Andy warmly congratulated me on my little promotion, and made me feel at ease right away; then he caught me a bit off guard by telling me I needed to improve my wardrobe, using my pal Andy Jansky as a role model for personifying the Executive Leasing Company sharp dressed image. Jansky always wore nice suits, had the power ties, the freshly starched button down dress shirts, and the cool penny loafers; a preppy look that was always popular with upper management.

As I sat there squirming in my ragamuffin outfit with my scuffed up shoes, I felt a little uneasy, but vowed that I'd invest in some nice suits and whatnot.

Andy again made me feel good about myself by telling me that after I came over to West County, the office really improved, administratively, and he was pretty sure it was because I was on top of things, such as making timely deposits, and making sure the cash box was balanced on a regular basis. I had to agree with him but I didn't think that was such a big deal; I'd just had a good background in that kind of stuff at South Kingshighway.

Of course, I was thinking to myself, Jansky was a selling machine, and his office generated huge profits, while South Kingshighway was better at making sure the money made it to the bank, but not necessarily huge sums of money; if you know what I mean.

Then Sheriff Taylor launched his final offensive, which again embarrassed me, but I took it in stride because I knew that would probably conclude the pep talk. Andy, with his oval face quite tanned and glistening, looked at me with a little disdain and said, "Larry, you need to get some sun. Don't you ever go outdoors? Get some color. You're too pale."

I nodded, as my head twitched with every lambasting sentence he bombarded me with; and vowed to nip it in the bud; I'd not only wear the right suits but also sit out and bake on a regular basis; yes sir, sometimes you've just got to nip it right in the bud, Andy.

I didn't want to belabor the fact that I hadn't been able to afford much golf to that point in my life, and I really hated going outside in the summer in St Louis unless I was engaged in some worthy activity, like golf.

Swimming always got on my nerves. While you're propped up or stretched out in some uncomfortable position, bagging those rays, it's not long until you're sweating your ass off in that wonderful St Louis heat and humidity, forcing you to jump in a potentially pool full of chlorine, urine and other miscellaneous pestilence to survive.

Eventually, you have to get out of the "water", and of course, that's quite an experience since the slightest breeze against your filthy, wet skin now creates the blissful feeling of being in Siberia in mid January. Shivering, as your teeth clatter together like castanets gone wild, you eventually dry yourself off just enough to feel uncomfortable with the heat and humidity again. I just don't get it. What price, vanity?

In the meantime, while you're broiling, you notice your skin is now painfully scorched, giving you a nice, red glowing aura; with enough doses of this therapy, maybe you'll get the look Andy was talking about. Then I was wondering, "Has Andy ever heard of skin cancer?"

At the conclusion of our heart to heart talk as I shook his sun-tanned hand, I thought to myself, "Andy's really a good guy. I'll try to make him proud of me." Over the next few years, I'd get to know him a little better, thanks to my frequent get-togethers with his sister, Jo Ann and her husband, Bob. I felt somewhat privileged to be hanging out with the Taylor clan, and I was always amazed at how down to earth both siblings were; because even way back then, they were just a little bit better off than the average millionaire.

Little did I know, in just a few years, I'd be opening Phoenix, Andy would be proud of me; and due to family matters beyond Andy's control, be stuck with his cousin, Pam, as my assistant manager. Nepotism would really rear its ugly head in earnest, I'd have to fire his cousin, but Andy would still be proud of me, because he even flew out to Phoenix to tell me so.

As I rose up the company ladder, I still regarded Andy Taylor as the same down to earth guy he was when I first got to know him. Aside from the slight bit of intimidation I felt when he gave me my little pep talk in '76, I felt as comfortable talking to him, as anybody else in the company, perhaps even more so, in many cases.

By the time my career had reached its peak, which happened to be my last year with the company, my relationship with this man had somehow changed; probably due to the fact that over the course of the years, as Enterprise grew to become the multi-billion dollar corporation that defines its essence today, Andrew C Taylor kept up with the times, and became the more serious President; while I remained the same old Uncle Larry.

This humble man; Jack's son Andy; had out of necessity, I suppose, become a somewhat ruthless head-honcho, which perhaps explains why everybody else around the nervous corporate office, treaded ever so delicately around the guy who ran the big show.

By the time my career had ended, I felt his animosity towards me, and that rankled me; I had always performed my duties with professionalism, although I was far from the typical Enterprise Officer; I kept a free-spirited, irreverent attitude; however, I suppose my refusal to become a clone created my downfall in the eyes on this now aging leader, and his number two man, an even older Don Ross.

I was certainly never a close, personal friend of Andy's, although we always seemed to have a cordial relationship; however, one of his old John Burroughs prep school cronies could seemingly get away with just about anything, being a FOA. This very notable General Manager, a good friend of Andy's, starting dating one of his branch rental managers, and made no bones about it; they were quickly married, and she became a former branch rental manager.

But these were the big '80s, and the company was small enough to fly under the radar screen of any possible sexual harassment issues, and nobody, including myself really thought much about it; it just seemed like another happy Enterprise love story.

Nowadays, however, it's one thing for a couple of Enterprise employees to meet on the job, develop a romantic relationship, and get married; it happens all the time (it happened to me); it's quite another thing for those two love birds be a General Manager and one of his employees. That shit just won't fly today.

Recently, a friend of mine asked me a rhetorical question; "Larry, if you were in charge of Enterprise Rent-a-Car, what would you do differently?"

I thought about it for about five seconds, and said, "Bob, I'd make five changes which I'd implement pretty much right away. In time, there may be some other things that would be worthy of change, but in all likelihood, nothing major; after all, this is the world's most successful car rental company."

Bob, a guy in his late '60s, had been a successful businessman himself, and we had mutual respect for each other. On this particular occasion, we were grabbing a little lunch at the 92nd Street Café, and as he was slicing up his steak, he leaned forward to hear my words of wisdom.

As I spoke, I laid the foundation for my decisions, and in a very logical manner, let him know the way things ought to be. Bob, as he slowly made his New York Strip disappear, intently looked me right in the eye, never blinking.

My first topic of discussion was my simple plan to cut back on the meetings, a real no brainer, as far as I was concerned.

General Managers currently are required to attend at least three annual meetings per year (since I've retired, maybe that number was increased, but I hope not for the sake of those poor souls). The meetings in May and October are tolerable, but some genius came up with the idea of having what is known as a "Mini GM Meeting", where a smaller group of General Managers gets to spend more quality time with Andy and the other head-honchos; and this meeting typically occurs in January or February in St Louis.

I'd get rid of that fucking mini-meeting immediately, saving the corporation millions of dollars annually on the expense of this brutal waste of time, and everybody would then be freed to get some actual work done (although St Louis is lovely that time of year).

Next, for God's sake, I'd let those poor employees (especially in the desert southwest) wear more comfortable attire when the temperatures reach that "inferno" level; for the sake of argument, beginning in May and ending in September, let them wear nice golf shirts (of course with that wonderful "e" logo) with nice slacks/skirts that would match the ensemble.

Color coordination would be simple; the golf shirts would be either red white or green; the slacks/skirts would be either khaki navy blue or gray. Any combination of shirts would match any combination of slacks/skirts; that's nine different ensembles for the happy Enterprise employees to wear; and even a color-blind employee would successfully look dapper in any combination of tops and bottoms.

The beauty of this wardrobe plan is that Enterprise could have its non-automotive Group (called the Capital Group) mass produce those golf shirts, sell them to the employees, and make a nice little profit in the process.

Number three on my hit list would be to simplify the long winded Enterprise "Mission Statement" they came up with in the early '90s; it's so fucking verbose it sounds more like a legal document than an inspiring piece of simple rhetoric to clearly let the employees know what Enterprise is all about as a company. Maybe they've already changed it; I don't know. If not, they really ought to consider doing so.

Taking a page from Wayne Kaufmann's "K.I.S.S. approach", the new and improved, simplified Mission Statement uses easy to follow "bullet points".

Here's how I'd word it:

"Our mission at Enterprise Rent-a-Car is to instill in every employee the understanding and desire to achieve our company's core values; this is the essence of what Enterprise truly represents:

*(S) Service to the customer above all else
*(H) Honesty and integrity in how we do business
*(O) Opportunity for advancement based on merit
*(T) Teamwork
*(S) Service to our communities; making them a better place to live

As we strive to fulfill these core values, please understand that it is our company policy to have fun while we work, and use acronyms at times like this, because they're so much fun; these are our 'S.H.O.T.S. of fun.'"

Now that's easy to remember and covers the important core values I believe Jack Taylor had in mind when he founded this company.

My next bold tactical maneuver, if I were the Chairman and Chief Executive Officer of this wonderful company, would be to simply lighten up. Show the employees in the trenches that I'm not such an intimidating guy; use a little humor every now and then, particularly when I'm giving a speech (Oh, don't sound like you're reading the speech, either; it sounds unprofessional).

Here's a true story; which happened a few years ago at the big rental managers meeting in Orlando. The company hired a fairly popular rock star from the late '90s to entertain the managers; it seemed like a good idea at the time; unfortunately, this once popular rock star had plummeted from being an A or B list star in his prime, to a C or D list rock star by the time he was hired by Enterprise; I think for something like fifty grand or so.

Well, this poor guy apparently had too much to drink or whatever, and he completely self destructed while giving his performance, spewing out expletives left and right, mocking Enterprise, while trying to babble about how wonderful Hertz was; it was a very embarrassing moment for everybody, and really, was quite sad.

The following morning, as Andrew C Taylor addressed the thousands of managers in attendance; who were still buzzing about the wild proceedings from the previous evening, very sternly began his speech as he pointed his right index finger in a very determined and presidential fashion; "I want to assure you all, that we will not give him one penny; not one penny; after his horrible behavior last night. Again, he will not get one penny!"

The embarrassed managers gave him the obligatory half hearted applause, but it wasn't what they wanted to hear from their fearless leader.

Andy, in his furor, missed the opportunity to turn what had happened into something a bit humorous, and consequently more beneficial to the overall morale of the managers who were now quizzically looking around at their cohorts smirking about the couple of pennies they would now be saving out of their next paycheck; big fucking deal.

I suppose if I were in charge, I would've said something like, "Hey, kids, if you want that guy's latest CD, I think K-Mart just marked it down to something like two cents." Big laugh from the crowd, and a grinning head-honcho is now a folk hero with those young kids in the trenches.

Or, I might've said, "Gosh, I was going to write that guy a check today to pay for his performance last night, but I just can't seem to locate my checkbook. I sure hope I find that darned thing." That whimsically gets the point across that he's not going to be getting one penny; not one penny!

Or, perhaps, "We agreed to pay that guy fifty grand; but maybe we should bump it to seventy-five grand, so he can get into a really good rehab program. I don't know; what do you guys think?" This tactic whimsically addresses the rock star's apparent substance abuse problem, and subtly conveys to the masses that maybe the guy's screwed up, but let's not make a federal case out of it.

The one liners are limitless and could serve a useful purpose in letting the managers in the field know that it's okay to screw up (as

Enterprise did by hiring that guy to begin with) so let's make fun of ourselves a little; quit pretending that Enterprise has never made a mistake; you can't fool the employees by putting on the pretense of being perfect; they know better, and trying to fool them will only cause disillusionment; which is already happening these days, from what I understand.

Of course, I'm not in charge of Enterprise, and if I had the job, I'd only want to keep it for a minimal amount of time; after I fired a few of the micro-managing drones scurrying around at corporate who seem to serve no purpose, except create more corporate overhead which all the managers in the field have to pay.

By giving the General Managers in the field greater autonomy, as Jack Taylor's original business plan absolutely mandated, a lot of corporate fat could be trimmed from the budget; the overall stress factor would be greatly reduced, thus creating better employee morale and a higher rate of employee retention.

That would conclude my five-step plan to make Enterprise a better place to work.

Obviously, Enterprise has done quite well in the eight years after my departure; the numbers seem to suggest they know exactly what they're doing (Well, before they acquired Alamo and National). My concern for this once fun-loving entrepreneurial company is they are distancing themselves from the real people in the field who are working very hard to make the company's long-winded Mission Statement a reality.

Ironically, many of these employees in the trenches are not really sure if accomplishing that will benefit their careers in the slightest.

In the final analysis, I suppose I think Andy's dad, Jack was more my kind of leader; the fact that the inevitable process of "age" gradually put Jack Taylor on the sidelines, makes me realize that while everything inexorably changes over time, those changes aren't always for the better.

Chapter 7
Making A Good (Lateral) Career Move

In the spring of 1980, I was finally starting to get a little restless with life as a branch rental manager. The familiarity that I loved four years earlier had faded away. Jo Ann Kindle was gone, raising a couple of young daughters as a stay at home mom. My favorite assistant manager was going to be leaving the company soon, as the whole leasing over rental syndrome was more than he could handle. He had just been promoted to manage the South Kingshighway office, after Ed had finally called it quits, in a move that was probably a mutual decision between upper management and Ed.

My buddy, Chuck Bader, was a straight shooting South County boy who had just married one of the St Louis Group's clerical personnel; a young, well endowed lady by the name of Carol Kennedy. The couple would go on to have four boys; one right after the other; with a set of twins thrown in for good measure. Carol eventually completed law school and became a district court judge in Crystal City, Missouri, the hometown of former New York Knicks Rhode Scholar turned senator and presidential hopeful, Bill Bradley. Chuck quit Enterprise and wound up having a nice career with Southwestern Bell.

Many years later, while Chuck and Carol were visiting Chuck's sister in Phoenix, I got together with them for lunch one day. During the course of the conversation, I had mentioned that we'd just received some sort of memo from corporate, pertaining to sexual harassment issues when Carol suddenly blurts out, "What a bunch of hypocrites!" Stunned, I just listened to her elaborate; it seems as though one very high-ranking corporate officer sexually harassed her on a regular basis, back in the late '70s. She told me who it was, but if I mentioned it here, I'd have to kill myself.

I'd better get back to the safety of 1980. That was the year I realized I shouldn't be married to the girl I married right out of college. However, coming from a dysfunctional, broken home (parents divorced when I was five, mother mentally ill) I vowed to make the marriage work, regardless of how I felt. Inevitably, things never really worked out, and three years later, I'd reluctantly get divorced, feeling like a complete failure.

In 1980, I felt like my life was heading towards failure, due to tough economic and emotional times. The commissions weren't happening for anybody and no relief was seen any time soon; I thought about quitting, but I suppose I just loved the business too much to throw away nearly six years of paying my dues; so I stuck it out.

One day, in the spring of that year, out of the blue, I got a call from Ed Bayer, an old boss I had at West County, who was now in charge of the St Louis Group. Ed told me that Group City Manager Don Marsh was taking a position with another part of the company which at the time was simply referred to as the non-automotive group; and that Dave Dieckmann would be taking over in the vacant City Manager slot. That meant the Clayton office would be available for me to take over, if I so desired. Initially, I turned it down; probably due to the general malaise I was going through; plus the fact that I considered it a lateral move, so why bother?

Then I came to my senses. I quickly called Ed back and accepted; after all, this was the glamour branch of St Louis, and even the entire company. I saw a tremendous amount of opportunity to show to the likes of Kaufmann and Brown that I was a real player; so I got my creative juices flowing again, and stormed into Clayton like Lawrence of Arabia.

I was having fun again, and I started putting up some strong numbers month in and month out. I think the corporate brain trust realized without a doubt that this artist still known as Uncle Larry was no fluke. Clayton usually led the Group, and at times, even the whole company, in all measurable areas of the business, and all I really did was capitalize on those rich lease customers who needed to rent cars from time to time. We sold everybody's ass up and made the whole process look very easy, because it really was easy.

Now I suppose I understood why all those managers were giving me congratulatory kudos at that 1980 spring rental manager's meeting; this high profile gig would be the springboard to my achieving much greater success, long-term. Everything was falling nicely into place, although at the time, I didn't realize how well into place things were so nicely falling; but in retrospect; it was very nice, indeed; yes, indeed.

As 1980 came to a close, I felt better about things, and looked forward to a Phoenix vacation I'd be taking with my wife in the latter part of January 1981. In the back of my mind, I was already picturing myself opening the newly established Phoenix Group, but I never thought making it happen would be so easy.

Chapter 8

Raising My Hand For Arizona

My trip to Phoenix in January 1981; convinced me that I'd found my new home; at least I hoped that would be the case. The second I got back to Clayton, I rushed over to Wayne Kaufmann's cubby hole of an office and casually mentioned I'd be willing to move to Phoenix any time Enterprise decided to open up there; actually, I kind of hollered it; not so casually.

A startled Kaufmann saw the look in my eyes, and knew I was dead serious; however, he was his usual noncommittal self, just saying, "So, you want to go to Phoenix, eh Larry?"

It seemed logical to open Phoenix on the heels of a very successful expansion into the Los Angeles, San Francisco, and Denver markets just a year prior; it also seemed logical to open Phoenix because that's where I wanted to live; isn't that reasonable?

Aware that things like this could take a while to develop, I didn't really give it much thought after that brief conversation with Wayne. I just went back to business as usual, as I usually did.

In the meantime, Pam Taylor, a young lady who happened to be Jack Taylor's niece, was getting her first dose of the rental business;

training in my branch. The original grand plan had Pam opening Tucson within the next few months, after completing the Uncle Larry Training Course.

However, after a couple of weeks, it was obvious that Pam wasn't going to be ready to open Tucson any time soon. She was indeed a Taylor, but that didn't mean she'd be able to learn the business practically overnight. In fact, there were those, myself included, who doubted Pam would ever really make it in the rental business at all. She seemed easily rattled, had trouble comprehending even the most basic concepts about the business, and didn't seem to have a very good work ethic.

Just months earlier, Pam's older sister, Carrie, had a disastrous stint with the newly formed San Francisco Group; and she left under very unpleasant circumstances. According to Lenny Alma, who was one of the top dogs in the Group, Carrie completely screwed up just about everything she did in her job, but upper management, fearing reprisals, decided not to fire her; instead, they deliberately made life unbearable for her by basically treating her like shit; and it certainly worked; she quit.

While Lenny was so proudly telling me this story about their clever handling of this delicate situation, I was thinking it didn't seem to be the way a business should deal with employee problems; and did he really think treating Carrie like shit might not cause problems, maybe even worse than the dreaded firing?

During the course of Carrie's younger sister's training, I let Kaufmann and Brown know that Pam was far from ready to handle the responsibilities associated with opening and running a new market. I had no idea what they might put together as an alternative plan, but I got wind of it around the middle of February, when my windbag assistant manager, Rick Goode, had some inside information he got from one of his cronies at corporate.

Rick always cocked his right eyebrow whenever he spoke, to add credibility to whatever tale he was telling. One frigid February morning, Rick pulled me aside and said, "Larry, I just got the inside scoop of what they're going to do with you and Pam." His eyebrow was cocked, dramatically, as he gave me the details. "They're going to open Phoenix first, and send you there with Pam as your assistant. After you get her trained, she'll move to Tucson."

I liked the part about me opening Phoenix; the rest of it, I didn't particularly care for. However, I wasn't going to worry about it, until I heard from Wayne or Doug; so I nodded my thanks to Rick whose eyebrow was still cocked, and again went back to business as usual, as I usually did, while I waited for that phone call.

A couple of weeks passed by when I received that phone call from Kaufmann. I knew right away what he was about to say; "Larry, are you still interested in opening Phoenix? Let's fly out there and find an office."

I agreed with the plan, which was just as Rick and his cocked eyebrow had tipped me off on a couple of weeks earlier.

When I met with Doug to finalize all the details, I let him know my concerns with Pam; "Doug, what if Pam doesn't pan out? What if she's not cut out for the rental business? How do we handle that?" Doug was already anticipating that question and was nodding his head as soon as I began that inquiry. He looked at me, took a drag from his cigarette, and said "Larry, just let me know when you've reached the end of your rope, and I'll handle it from there", blowing smoke in my face.

That was all I could ask for. Doug would take the heat from the Taylors for me; and really, I didn't think Jack or Andy would be overly surprised or disappointed. It was Pam's father, Paul, whose wrath I feared the most. I'm sure he was counting on me to get his daughter up to speed, and if that failed, he would be getting Pam's spin on how horrible I was to work for; and how unfair I was.

Having already mentally prepared for the worst-case scenario, I decided to keep an open mind, and do everything in my power to make Pam Taylor a valued Enterprise manager. I knew one thing for sure; if Pam didn't work out, I wasn't going to use the San Francisco Group "treat them like shit method" for getting rid of an unsatisfactory employee. Holy shit.

Since I wasn't a leasing guy, Doug made it clear to me to not get any wild ideas; this wasn't a promotion to General Manager. Although I was opening this new market by myself, there would come a time when a General Manager would come in over me. I didn't worry about that; my only concern was doing a good job, making some profit for the corporation, and trying to somehow pull off the impossible miracle of getting Pam Taylor trained, ready and able, to go off on her own to open Tucson. Holy shit.

My salary for the first year was to be a guaranty of $24,000, which was about what I was making running the Clayton branch. That seemed fair; and off to Phoenix Wayne and I went to find that first Arizona branch.

Chapter 9

The Worst Case Taylor Nepotism Scenario

Wayne Kaufmann and I stormed into Phoenix at the end of March, combed the Valley of the Sun for a suitable office to call "home", and settled for a spot in Mesa; formerly a Winchell's Donut Shop.

The two days I spent riding around that rental car with Wayne were agonizing. Wayne insisted on listening to country music, which I generally hated, and thought it would be amusing to fart every time he got into the car, and then about every five or ten minutes afterwards, just to keep me alert. Wayne seemed to be enjoying himself, so I felt happy for him.

Just to make sure I was being tortured sufficiently, he'd groan about the "heat"; wondering why anybody in their right mind, would ever want to live in a horrible place like this? It was in the mid seventies every day and I told Wayne to have fun shoveling that fucking snow next January. We laughed and laughed.

Our triumphant return to St Louis coincided with a birthday party Andy Taylor was hosting for his cousin Pam, my soon-to-be assistant manager. In a couple of months, we'd both be sweltering in the desert heat, trying to get some business from wherever we could find it; but on this particular occasion we were celebrating another birthday for the birthday girl, while raising our glasses time and time again to toast the future success of the Phoenix Group. That night, optimism reigned supreme; the next day, it was back to reality.

That April was a bittersweet month for me in Clayton. I was looking forward to the move to Phoenix, but was getting sentimental about the good times I'd had in St Louis, and knew I was going to miss the whole routine; and most of all, miss the people.

The future seemed so uncertain; I didn't know anything about ordering cars, hiring people, getting contractors lined up to remodel the donut shop; not to mention, going into a brand new market where nobody would ever know anything about Enterprise Rent-a-Car. It was entrepreneurialism in its purest form, except I was playing with Enterprise's $50,000, not mine.

In early May; in preparation for my permanent move to Phoenix, I camped out at the corporate offices for a week or so and had crash courses in everything I didn't know anything about. I'm not sure how much information I really digested, but I thought, what the fuck; what I don't know, I'll fake.

In mid May, I arrived in Phoenix, greeted by what seemed to be a blast furnace as I stepped on to the scorching tarmac at Sky Harbor International Airport. It was well over 100 and my thoughts went out to Wayne Kaufmann, wishing he were here. My first year in the Valley of the Blast Furnace turned out to be the hottest summer on record. Coincidentally, it seems like every summer is the newest hottest summer on record. In fact, as I type this, in the year 2008, it's the hottest summer on record.

If anybody has any doubt about global warming, just try melting in Phoenix for the summer; it's the new way to vacation; the new way to have everything you've always wanted in an inferno but were afraid to ask.

The rest of that month was spent lining up contractors, getting in touch with employment agencies, and marketing our services to all the insurance companies and insurance agents in town, placing emphasis on the fact that our Mesa location is ideal for anybody in the east valley. Our main competitor at the time was American International Rent-a-Car, and everybody seemed to like them, but they were all the way down by the airport. We got our foot in the door with a lot of accounts simply by having a convenient location for the folks in Mesa, Tempe, Chandler, and Gilbert; areas that were just starting explode with growth.

Some of the Chevys that we'd placed on order a month earlier were starting to trickle in by the middle of June. In the meantime, much to my surprise, I had some good candidates who were interested in actually working for Uncle Larry's Rent-a-Car.

The first person I hired was Jim Loomer, who would eventually become a big shot General Manager in the early '90s, before retiring a couple of years after I rode off into the Sunset Station casino. I liked Jim; he did quite well for me, and essentially surpassed Pam on the learning curve less than a month into the job. In a relatively short period of time, Pam was routinely going to Jim for answers whenever she had issues she didn't know how to handle. Jim would say, "Larry; she's the assistant; right?"

Business was starting to pick up nicely as July rolled into August, and with Jim acting as de-facto assistant manager, we were in pretty good shape. Pam clearly felt better about not having to assume much responsibility, and did a pretty good job of marketing the dealerships, especially in the Scottsdale area.

Jim and I developed pretty good relations with the predominantly Mormon State Farm and Farmers agents in the east valley. We put two and two together one day, and realized for the most part, they thought we were Mormons as well. We never brought up the subject when we were calling on these accounts, but with the white shirts and conservative ties we wore as part of the "Enterprise look", we certainly fit right in with the rest of the clan.

As the summer rolled into fall, Pam's work ethic really began slipping. For the weekends, she'd either drive down to Tucson to visit her parents, or on occasion, she'd fly to San Francisco, to party with her sister. Her absences from work on the Mondays after her San Francisco weekends were becoming a problem; the volume of business, and the vast amount of territory we had to cover, made it imperative to have everybody report to work, bright eyed and bushy tailed; especially on Mondays. When we were understaffed, we'd have a tough time taking care of customers, and as a result, we were having some credibility issues with some of our accounts.

Consequently, whenever Pam would sneak into the office in the wee hours Monday mornings, after a weekend of revelry in San Francisco, to leave me a note saying she was "too exhausted" to work that day, we'd have trouble doing our jobs proficiently.

Even on the days she'd show up for work, she'd perform her duties haphazardly, and all kinds of problems ensued. It was obvious Pam really didn't like working for Enterprise, and by January 1982, the problem had come to a head. I called Doug Brown and said I'd had it with Pam; it wasn't working and there wasn't a chance in hell that it ever would work. Doug didn't hesitate, saying, "Don't worry, Larry; I'll let Andy know."

With that phone call, the life of Pam Taylor improved dramatically. She was free from the shackles of having to work in a business she had no desire to work in; and I was glad to take the blame if Pam told her father I was the bad guy.

However, Paul Taylor had a personal stake in the Phoenix Group; although he probably allowed paternal instincts to side with his daughter initially; he would soon have a change of heart; in January we made our first profit, and with each passing month, the bottom line kept getting stronger. By May, we were strong enough financially, to open our second office.

Chapter 10

Phoenix Gets A General Manager, Enterprise Loses Its Finest

W ith Pam Taylor's permanent departure from the company, things around the office got hectic again; almost like the days when Pam was resting at home after a long weekend of boogying in San Fran. I hired a couple of new guys; Steve Downs, who would prove to be a bust in the long run, and Ed Player, who worked out well for me, but ran into trouble when he took a promotion outside the Group in the early '90s; but they were still wet behind the ears, so Jim and I were trying our best to keep things together.

Almost immediately after Pam was fired, Andy Taylor rushed out to Phoenix to console me. I think he just wanted to let me know there were no hard feelings, and that I wasn't in the dog house with him or his father; in fact, he didn't think the plan was going to work either, but had to go along with it for the sake of Uncle Paul, who was trying to get his daughters into some sort of productive career type mode.

He really seemed embarrassed by the whole fiasco, but I knew his hands were tied by the family situation. It was no big deal; and the fact that Pam landed a bartending job in Tucson which led to meeting her future husband and father to maybe a couple of kids (at least one for sure), I'm sure everybody in the Taylor family realized that Uncle Larry helped make it all happen; what a guy.

That was the last time Andy ever personally visited me, as the company was starting to grow, exponentially, and he would just be too tied up with the duties of his job to make little side trips to visit guys like me. At any rate, that was a very class act for the man known as A.C.T. (For you Enterprise trivia buffs, Andy's middle name is the same as his father, J.C.T.---Crawford.)

Meanwhile, the snowbirds were flocking to Arizona, and we were really scrambling to handle the tremendous influx of business that occurred during the first three months of the year. It was great from a business perspective, but it was definitely nerve-wracking at the same time. Still, we were now a viable entity in the company, and now worthy of opening a second office; which at the time seemed like a big deal.

In order to open that second office, I was going to need major help. Assuming I'd temporarily set up shop at the new branch, I was going to need somebody with experience to stabilize the original office, and lend knowledge and leadership to the relatively new crew of employees in both offices.

It was time to add a General Manager.

A year earlier, when I accepted Doug Brown's offer to be City Manager of the Phoenix Group, it came with the understanding that I wouldn't become a General Manager any time soon; so when the time came to add somebody, it would be someone out of their usual talent pool of leasing candidates. As luck would have it, Larry Snow wasn't available, but I got Jim Keene instead, which was almost as good.

My phone call to Doug Brown, shortly before we were getting ready to open that second branch, on the west side of town (Glendale) conveyed a sense of urgency that we needed somebody to step up to the plate very soon. Doug sprang into action and within a few days called back to cheerfully report that he found our man (there still were no women running groups yet; nor minorities for that matter).

As Doug was inhaling his cigarette, he'd start talking; "Larry, there's a guy from Kansas City by the name of Jim Keene who's done a great job there and would love the chance to move out to Phoenix." Doug then exhaled his tar and nicotine. He continued; "Jim's just a big, friendly guy with a positive attitude, and I'm sure he'd do a great job out there getting the leasing business off the ground, as well as provide the necessary leadership to help you and your new people grow your business."

I had no idea that was his way of saying, "There's a very good chance this guy's going to suck so take it or leave it."

I vaguely remembered Jim Keene before he moved to Kansas City, when he was a lease salesman back in St Louis; I remember seeing him a time or two at the North office but we never spoke, and that was about the extent of my exposure to big Jim Keene.

Since I knew absolutely nothing about the guy other than the fact he was a big burly white fellow, I thanked Doug for getting someone lined up so quickly, and that I certainly looked forward to meeting big Jim Keene, the leasing machine from Kansas City; the great big show, from KC, MO.

Big Jim and his appropriately sized wife, Karen arrived on the scene a few days later all dressed up in their big old suits; looking very uncomfortable in the late April warmth, which signaled the start of another hellish summer.

I think they were kind of overwhelmed by the whirlwind manner in which they were plopped into their new Group. I'm sure it must've been quite a culture shock to leave the safety and serenity of the prosperous Kansas City Group, with their lovely offices and fat commissions to come to this pathetic little one office Group, with that one office being a remodeled donut shop who many people thought was still actively in the business of serving those yummy pastries; and there was, of course, absolutely no leasing business on the books yet.

As Jim and Karen sat there with their pained, forced smiles on their more than slightly perspiring faces, I thought to myself, "They don't look very comfortable with the situation; and Jim sure does have a huge head."

I tried to make them feel at ease, by giving them a quick overview of what was going on, hoping that Jim would interject something of substance, and we could have a nice business conversation, or something. It was weird, but no matter what I said, Jim would instantly reply, "Super!" Apparently, that was the word that he thought he should use at least a hundred times a day, because deep down inside, I knew not everything I said was really all that super.

I'm not sure what super Jim's plan was to get the leasing business off the ground; I'm not sure Jim knew what his plan was going to be, because he didn't seem to do anything super along those lines when he showed up for work. That wasn't my concern; I was just hoping he'd write up a few rental contracts for us and answer a few phone calls; and he did. I was hoping for a superstar, but I'd settle for a warm body; well, I guess a great big super warm body.

Naturally, Jim had the usual mindset of the leasing prima donna. The only problem was, leasing didn't mean shit at this point; the Phoenix Group was 100% rental, and the profits generated were from rental, not leasing. When I was working in St Louis, "Enterprise Leasing" just rolled off your tongue; somehow it sounded right. In Phoenix, that sounded stupid and confusing; so we answered the phones, "Enterprise Rent-a-Car"; that's right; Enterprise Rent-Not-Lease-a-Fucking Car; holy shit; calm down, Uncle Larry.

Since Jim's biggest contribution was answering the phones when our guys were tied up with customers, he used to delight in droning, "Enterprise Leasing"; and it drove me crazy. In turn, I relished answering the phone, "Enterprise Rent-a-Car"; and in the corner of my eye I could see him glaring at me with those steely brown leasing eyes.

Technically, I suppose he was right, although he never told me to change my evil ways. Every now and then, just to show big Jim I was a team player, I'd hastily answer the phone, "Enterprise Rent-a-Car (oops) and Leasing", but I think that really pissed him off even more because he thought I was being sarcastic; and looking back on it, I suppose I was. The official name change operation wouldn't take place until the end of the decade, but as far as I was concerned the operation had already been performed in Phoenix.

The timing for Jim's arrival in Phoenix was actually quite good; I had to head out to St Louis to attend the annual rental managers meeting, so at least big super Jim could take care of any situation while I was away. In the meantime, Doug Brown decided to let Jim's promotion go unannounced to the company, which was somewhat unusual, I thought, but perhaps he wanted to break the news to the rental guys first.

What happened during the first day of meetings was inadvertently hilarious, the way everything played out; and as luck would have it, I was right in the middle of it.

These meetings were something I really looked forward to, as some of my favorite rental guys were from places like Orlando, Denver, St Louis, and of course, Houston; which is where my old buddy Andy Jansky was now residing.

During the first day, everybody's just making a little small talk with other colleagues; and I could tell by the tone of the idle conversation, nobody had a clue about the arrival of Jim Keene from Kansas City to boss me around in Phoenix, and I wasn't going to spill the beans; I knew the subject would somehow pop up during the course of the meeting.

The murmur of idle conversation and occasional laughter slowly faded as the managers chose their seats and prepared to start ripping into Doug Brown, almost immediately, as the meeting officially began.

It didn't take long for the discussion to shift to the controversial "leasing over rental syndrome" as a beleaguered Doug Brown wearily defended the argument that it only made sense to have the leasing guys in charge, since after all, "That's just the way it is."
I knew all too well, "that's just the way it is", as my thoughts went out to big Jim Keene from Kansas City taking over the reigns in Phoenix, where leasing would surely reign supreme, because "that's just the way it's always been".

As I looked around the room, I saw the intensity in the faces some of the city managers who had been in their positions for a lot longer than me, and were really getting tired of that time-honored bullshit tradition.

Three guys were really letting "the Brown man" have it; my good friend, Andy Jansky, Dave Willey, an old St Louis pal of mine who helped open the Southern California Group in 1980, and a good old boy from Orlando, Dick Rush.

Very early in the debate, Dick thought it would be perfect to use my unique scenario to hammer home his point; as he first eyeballed me, I had a pretty good idea what was going to happen next.

Dick quickly snapped his head in the direction of the wary Doug Brown, who was in the process of lighting up another cigarette and seemed startled by Dick's intimidating head jerk; "Doug; you mean to tell me, that Larry Underwood, who got Phoenix going all on his own, could have some 'Joe Blow' leasing guy come in there and take over?"

Of course, that not only could happen, it did happen. I thought I'd spare Doug the embarrassment of now having to announce that Joe Blow, also known as Jim Keene, the super-leasing guy, was now the General Manager of the Phoenix Group.

I never even gave Doug a chance to utter a word, as I spontaneously blurted, "He's there!" I had a devilish grin on my face, signaling to my colleagues that even though I knew this was a silly decision, I wasn't worried about it; after all, that's just the way it is.

There was a brief pause, as everyone's mouth dropped open; this moment reminded me of the time Larry Snow told everybody in our office to not rent any cars because it was too dangerous. Then came the inevitable roar of laughter as everybody looked at Rush, who was so flabbergasted he couldn't speak; and then he started laughing, too, while shaking his head in disbelief.

Over the years, I'd call this the "Enterprise guffaw", a blend of real and fake laughter that everyone feels compelled to do, simply because the moment seemed appropriately significantly humorous; and this moment certainly fit that bill.

This guffawing moment epitomized the antiquated logic that pervaded the ranks of the upper echelon of the company. Enterprise had always revolved around the world of leasing; but now the upstart rental division was getting very loud and boisterous; and packing some clout. The tide was turning; within the next four years, three of us would become General Managers; Dave Willey, Dick Rush, and then me.

Certainly, had Andy Jansky lived long enough, he would've been the first to move up. I remember glancing over at Andy while the cramped, smoke-filled meeting room was erupting with guffawing laughter; and even though he too was laughing, I could see the look of fury in his eyes, as he pondered the inequity of the situation.

Gradually, as the laughter died down, Andy fixed a stare straight ahead at nothing in particular, still no doubt thinking, as he so often said, "This is bullshit."

Doug Brown who was also smiling, but looked a bit frazzled, gave me a wink, and adjourned the meeting for a ten-minute break, so he could regroup and let everybody else wind down. I smiled and gave him the knowing nod.

As the riled up managers lit up cigarettes of their own and waded into the men's room, the jovial rumbling from what had just transpired persisted. When I took my turn, none other that Dick Rush was washing his hands with his freshly lit cigarette dangling from his mouth. He looked at me, grinning and said, "Damn, Underwood; I had no idea some leasing asshole had already taken over there! That is fucked up, man!" His cigarette was bouncing up and down as he spoke, seemingly having some sort of conniption fit; and that seemed appropriate.

He was right. It was fucked up; but what could I do? I just went along with it and hoped that sooner or later, the mindset of the company would change.

In retrospect, I believe the mindset of the company changed in the aftermath of that one significant, guffawing meeting. With the daily rental department's burgeoning growth, clearly the leadership of the company was shifting in that direction; and this new talent pool was getting restless.

The Sunday after that meeting, Andy Jansky, Dave Dieckmann, Dave Willey, and I met at Steak 'n Shake for a quick burger before we headed back to our respective cities. In the '70s, we all worked in the St Louis Group, and for a while, Andy, Dave Willey and I worked together at the West County office. Now with only Dieckmann still in St Louis, I realized that this little company was starting to grow in all directions, and its talent pool was getting ready for prime time.

In years past, the rental guys would grouse about the system, and wonder if things would ever change. This year, we seemed to realize that finally, things would start changing, very soon. This quartet of rental guys was now hungry for those world famous steak burgers, incomparable fries, and true flavor shakes; not concerned about business matters this year, at all.

With the peace of mind that comes from knowing life is good, the conversation shifted to baseball. Dieckmann and I were the biggest Cardinal fans, and we both optimistically chirped about the game the night before, when St Louis pulled one out of the fire against a tough Atlanta team.

Jansky chimed in, joking as he always did, about some ballplayer he thought had a humorous name; in the '70s he'd always mention the name of Cardinals outfielder Jerry Mumphrey, simply because he liked the way "Mumphrey" sounded in the usual Andy Jansky elongated way; this time, it was Enos Cabell, who played third base for the Astros; Andy's adopted team. With Andy's elongated pronunciation of "Cabell", it took a good five seconds for him to finish; of course, the bonus with that name came from the humorous way Andy crooned "Enos".

As usual, his routine cracked me up, while Andy smiled contentedly; soon, we started a rambling diatribe highlighted by a hilarious debate over who was the better third baseman; Enos Cabell or Ken Oberkfell? By this time, the two Daves were wondering if Andy and Larry really thought this was funny; but we had some of the other patrons of Steak 'n Shake rolling in the aisles as the rhyming debate raged; Cabell or Oberkfell? Being in St Louis, I used the home court advantage to my favor, asking the bemused patrons the rhetorical question; whom would you rather have on third base; Cabell, or Oberkfell? The inevitable response was weighted heavily in favor of the Cards' slick fielding, soft .300 hitting third-sacker, our hero, Kenny Oberkfell, while Janksy feigned mock indignation.

Afterwards, as we all said our "goodbyes", Andy gave me the expected good-natured ribbing about my new boss, and leasing in general, and of course, I cracked up again, while shaking his hand for that last time.

Walking towards my gate as he headed in another direction towards his gate, we both turned, made good-natured eye contact, nodded, and gave each other the quick "see you later" wave as we were preparing for our journeys from Lambert International Airport to our now familiar Enterprise expansion cities.

Andy had already proven himself with his accomplishments in Houston, and I was only starting to get things going in Phoenix; however, I felt good about the future, and confident that things would fall into place, as they always had in the past.

I was still smiling when I boarded that TWA flight for Phoenix, contentedly reflecting on the significance of the events that took place during that first hilarious day of meetings. "Finally", I thought, "Rental is no longer such a bad department, after all", a mocking tribute to the upcoming, inevitable rise, in respectability that would be happening very soon; and I concluded to myself, trying to squelch a laugh, "I'd take Oberkfell over Cabell any day as my third baseman." A flight attendant gave me a bewildered look, since she didn't think anything was very funny at that particular moment; I just smiled and shrugged my shoulders, as if to say, "It's okay; it's only me."

Andy Jansky, as chipper as he was on that Sunday in early May 1982, playing the baseball player name game that he seemingly patented, while the four lifetime rental guys devoured Steak 'n Shake's finest during that hilarious mock debate featuring a couple of third basemen named Cabell and Oberkfell; I knew he felt good about the future as well.

Sadly, that would be the last time I'd see Andy alive; I'd be back in St Louis just three weeks later to attend his funeral.

Chapter 11

The Speech Heard 'Round The Enterprise World

Returning from the funeral of Andy Jansky, I felt drained; still grieving from the loss of a good friend, and my tolerance for bullshit was at an all-time low. I would soon turn 30, and still being young and immature; felt old. Without a doubt, my sullen behavior carried over to my life at home with a wife I really should've never married. We were never really that close to begin with, and now we were quite happy going in different directions for our social endeavors. Despite a trip to Hawaii in February of 1983, there was no spark going on between us at all; and by April, she was gone.

Somehow, her decision to call it quits came as an unwelcome revelation, and for a period of a week or two, I was miserable, feeling like a complete loser. Luckily, I didn't have time to feel sorry for myself; our third office had just opened up in Central Phoenix, with a very catchy address; 1111 E Camelback, and a very catchy phone number; 265-1111; so I temporarily stationed myself here to get it up and running.

Big Jim Keene and I were so proud of ourselves; we had what we considered to be a real showcase office with the cool address and phone number; however, we soon realized that UPS once had that cool phone number; because 90% of the time, when the phone rang, we'd get somebody who wanted to ship a package back home to Aunt Betty and Uncle George.

The process of trying to re-educate the greater Phoenix area to the new phone number and address for UPS, got to be a laborious and painstaking one. Just when we thought we'd gotten over the hump, the Holiday season began, and all hell broke loose again. The people who spent any amount of time at that branch, to avoid total insanity, would have a little fun with it every now and then. I overheard one of the guys talking to somebody who wanted a package shipped somewhere; and he'd inquire, "Where to? How much does it weigh? Let's see; that'll be $800."

With a straight face, I said, "Ken, you guys are getting expensive."

That reminds me of when our first little office opened up in Mesa, on the corner of Main and Dobson---between Denny's and Wendy's.. For years, it was a Winchell's Donut Shop; so most of the people who waddled in there, especially before we even had our sign up, thought it still was a donut shop, and damned if they still didn't want a donut even after we told them they had the wrong place. The look of indignation on some people's faces was hysterical. Somehow, it was our fault that Winchell's was no longer here.

After a while, Jim Loomer and I would make bets on whether the people ambling towards our door wanted a donut or a car, playing the new game "Car or Donut?" Usually, they wanted the donut; so we developed a very quick routine to get them back on the right track; "No we rent cars here. Winchell's is now located down the street, just past Country Club. You're welcome; now get your fat ass out of here."

My favorite incident occurred when a nice, elderly, gentleman walked in; took a quick look around at the shirts and ties we adorned, and immediately came to the conclusion that we were the administrative headquarters for Winchell's Donuts. He peeped his head inside the office, not wanting to disturb our donut analysis reports, and very politely asked, "Where's your closest location?" I just looked up, smiled, and said "Just past Country Club, sir." He smiled and nodded his appreciation. I never lost my smile and gave him the knowing nod as well, before I got back to the business of glazed donuts and chocolate crème filled donuts.

Then I wondered when our fucking sign would ever be ready, as the smile slowly dissipated.

Meanwhile, back at the ranch; as I was getting myself prepared for my upcoming trip to my old home town to attend the annual rental managers meeting, I thought I'd look through my phone list to see if anybody's name just popped out for me to call.

When I was working in St Louis a few years earlier, I became friends with a very attractive and outgoing divorcee, who worked for an insurance company we did some business with; named Cindy Constantine. Cindy and her fellow workers were kind enough to give me a little going away present, as I headed off to open Phoenix in '81, which I still have, a little plastic nameplate calling me "Larry Underwear".

Being newly divorced myself, I decided to look her up and see what was shaking; secretly, I'd always had a bit of a crush on her, so now seemed like a good time to see if there were any mutual feelings.

I met her for dinner at some Italian restaurant in the "Hill" section of South St Louis, and the next thing I knew, I was completely smitten by this beautiful woman, and was mentally preparing for an unrealistic long distance love affair. The next night would be the start of the rental meeting, and I was psyched, feeling good about my career and my apparent blossoming love life.

Although several of my buddies were trying to console me over my recent divorce, they quickly surmised that I really didn't need any consoling at all; in fact, I was downright giddy. They could tell by the twinkle in my eye that I wasn't wasting time feeling sorry for myself; and they very quickly lost that sympathetic look in their eyes.

Wayne Kaufmann had sprung a little surprise for those attending the rental managers meetings, shortly before we were to head to the Gateway city.

Much to the dismay of many and the delight of very few, for the first time ever, the poor city managers had to give a speech to all those in attendance about all of the exciting things happening in their towns, from a rental perspective. Boy, I could hardly wait to hear everybody's report and was certainly looking forward to giving my presentation. The fever pitch of excitement was so intense I could hardly contain myself. All the fellows were really getting pumped up about the chance to really shine in front of Wayne, and all those important Officers who work at corporate; which of course, is a totally bullshit spin on this madness; the fever pitch of excitement; that sounded good, though.

Actually, nobody that I talked to thought this was such a good idea; and in fact, many of the future orators were so nervous the supply of toilet paper in St Louis suddenly became dangerously low; scientists have discovered that 97 people out of 100 really hate giving speeches, and even imaging the audience is naked only makes it worse in most cases, especially with that particular Enterprise crowd; causing severe stomach cramps, and worse, permanent emotional distress.

My wretched roommate for this meeting, little Brad from Kansas City (who of course, knew big Jim Keene), was so distraught about the prospects of public speaking that I seriously thought he had some sort of intestinal disease. He spent more time on the throne than Henry VIII; while I tried to find refuge in some small portion of that tiny hotel room that wouldn't stink; in order to prepare for my upcoming debacle. I was planning on making this travesty short and sweet, so I could dash back to my seat and get back to being invisible while the others withstood their five minutes of shame, right there in the spot light of the ostentatious St Louis Club.

The speeches were even more unbearable than I possibly imagined. The city managers were either so nervous, they could barely make it through the presentation without having a complete nervous breakdown; or they were such self absorbed windbags that they couldn't stop talking about how wonderful they were. Kaufmann seemed to be the only one listening to these speeches at all, from what I could surmise; and that was probably only because this whole mess was his fucking idea.

The first night of terror ended, with only about half of the victims being thrown to the lions. I was forced to wait, I thought, just to punish me for being happy. I really wasn't as much nervous as I was agitated to be subjected to such cruel and unusual punishment. This was even worse than having to ride around with Wayne all day long in a car, listening to country music, while trying to get a breath of fresh air as his farts incessantly flew, without warning.

During the increasingly repetitious bullshit that was being doled out by the second round of victims, I sat there with my little cocktail napkin in hand, mentally rehearsing how I was going to ad lib those cryptic notes I had scribbled on this tiny shred of damp, paper-like material. As I sat there stewing, I'd flag down a waiter from time to time to get some more of that wonderful wine they were serving. I'm sure the people who were seated at my little table were thinking what a complete dick this guy from Phoenix appeared to be.

Suddenly, with only another three or four victims remaining to be tortured, I could hear Wayne wearily drone, "Here to tell you what's going on in Phoenix is Larry Underwood." As I confidently strode to the podium, I could almost hear a couple people in the audience pretend to applaud my presence. For the most part all I heard was the dull murmur of desperate people trying to converse with their buddies what they were going to do after they escaped this wretched zombie-like enclave called the St Louis Club.

When I ended my death march to the podium, I suddenly felt at ease; not like I was having an out-of-body experience or anything; but it felt cool to be propped up in front of a real, live microphone, as hundreds of beleaguered spectators disdainfully looked on. For some reason I can't explain, I decided to act like a complete lunatic, hoping to receive a favorable response from this surly gathering. It worked.

For absolutely no good reason, I started off with this killer opening line: "Now batting for Pedro Borbon; Manny Mota." The frazzled audience, including those poor waiters, waitresses, and bus boys, exploded with raucous laughter. I acted like I wasn't totally shocked by the favorable response; but of course I was; and I was grateful that the movie "Airplane!" had supplied me with that all-important ice-breaking gag.

After the laughter died down a bit, I just hunched over the microphone and said, "Sorry; I always wanted to be a P.A. announcer." Hell, they even thought that was funny. Now I was thinking to myself, "They'll laugh at anything." But the truth of the matter was, I always dreamed of being the guy to introduce the Cardinals fans' favorite players just because it would be so much fun to strategically accentuate whatever syllables in that player's name that would cause the maximum amount of pandemonium.

For some reason, the St Louis Club was now in a state of pandemonium, and I must've been butter, because I was on a roll; I then launched into a hilarious routine; lampooning everything we'd been subjected to, up to this point; capping it off with a recount of our brave struggle in Phoenix with the horrible weather we had to endure, like the terrifying day 1/16 of an inch of rain fell, making it oh so difficult to get to work; I mean, we had to turn the windshield wipers on and everything.

The audience loved it, which only proves how desperate they were for anything even remotely humorous; and luckily for me, Jack Taylor, who bore a striking resemblance to Steve Martin, and the rest of the corporate big wigs really got a kick out of it. I suppose if the corporate hierarchy didn't have a sense of humor, I might've been out of work by the following Monday; but these were the fun-loving '80s, and the climate was right for a little Uncle Larry levity; besides, I thought Steve Martin would like it.

Upon completion of my monologue I felt like a rock star. Young managers from all over the country were coming up to me telling me how wonderful I was, and shaking my hand. It was almost embarrassing, but I dealt with it.

Later that evening, the girl of my dreams, Cindy Constantine, stopped by the hotel for a brief visit before I would head back to Phoenix. As we strolled into the hotel bar and through the lobby, my rock star status rose even higher; I could hear the comments about me being with this hot babe, and feel the stares as I casually had my arm around her. It was a surrealistic moment for me, and I hoped the feeling would never end.

Apparently, all good things must come to an end. Although my career was now solidly locked into the fast track, my love life fizzled; Cindy didn't want to get involved in any sort of long distance relationship and she sure as hell didn't want to move to Phoenix.

Chapter 12

Becoming An Overnight Sensation After Ten Years

I tried to shrug off my latest romantic debacle, but I had known this woman for a long time, and even though we had never really been romantically involved before, I sure as hell wanted to head in that direction now. We remained friends, and I tried to get a spark going with her from time to time over the course of the next two years, but nothing ever quite materialized, long term; and that would be that.

The guys I used to hang out with from work after a long day in the trenches may have sensed the malaise I was experiencing, and they'd invite me to join them for cocktails on a regular basis; or they just wanted me around to pick up the tab.

Our little happy hours were a blast. Every now and then, we'd take some insurance companies out for happy hours, and darned if that didn't strengthen our rapport with these accounts, as we all happily got plowed.

After a while, we started hitting a place called "Fantasy World", a very popular gentlemen's club in those days. The ringleader for this activity was a free spirited guy by the name of Dick Jansen who I really liked, although he seemed a little shady at times. Dick would call to tell me we would be holding an "Audubon Society" meeting at the usual place, and would then go into some spiel about a particular bird with ruffled feathers on its breast that would be the focus of our study that particular evening. He always cracked me up, in much the same manner as Andy Jansky's antics a few years prior.

The dancers at Fantasy World loved us. We were a motley crew, with our strange looking long-sleeved white shirts and ties very loosened around our sweaty necks, but always polite, fun-loving, and generous; in time, we knew every dancer by name; and they not only knew our names but developed a fondness for some of our ties. I had to give a few of my ties honorable discharges after their tour of duty at "The World".

Eventually, when Dick called, he'd simply say, "The birds will flock."

The birds stopped flocking within a couple of months. Our old familiar hangout closed up without warning one evening, and six guys from Enterprise remorsefully looked around that parking lot, wondering what happened. We tried other establishments, but they just weren't the same. The "Audubon Society" summer of '83 was over.

Those silly escapades helped create a sense of camaraderie in that small, close-knit group of Enterprise employees. Everybody seemed to enjoy hanging out together, knowing they were among friends. Those were simpler times, when it was easy to trust one another. There were no hidden agendas, just a lot of laughs.

The corporate hierarchy really loved me now, as the Phoenix Group was starting to post some strong numbers, and my killer one-night stand at the St Louis Club gave me instant star power credibility. In fact, they loved me so much they thought I was ready for "prime time" by December of 1983; I was actually offered a promotion to become a General Manager, and I was actually dumb enough to turn it down.

I was offered Seattle and rejected it for several reasons; none of which were any good. The primary stupid reason I used, thinking it sounded very good, was, "I've only been in Phoenix for two years, and there's so much more I want to accomplish here." In other words, what I was really saying was, "I'm single now, I'm getting laid on a regular basis, and I don't want to go through the bullshit of having to open a brand new market where it rains all the time and I don't even know anybody. Okay?"

For some reason, the corporate hierarchy still liked me. I just waved off a promotion like some asshole leasing prima donna rejecting his free ride home that night saying the Gremlin he had been given to drive "just doesn't look right"; and somehow, they still liked me. My irrational thinking was, "I want to land a promotion somewhere in the desert southwest."

"Now go away, and don't come back until you have something really splendid to offer. I shan't be happy with you unless all my wishes are fulfilled. Go away, I said; go!"

"Certainly; as you wish, Mr. Uncle Larry, sir. We won't be bothering you with any more nonsense; we're terribly sorry for the inconvenience, and we'll work on something very splendid for you; very splendid, indeed!"

"Whatever; oh, and while you're at it; I need to examine the list of fair maidens in the, uh kingdom. I think I fancy a fine young, lass who has mirth and merriment in her heart, and a siren's voluptuous endowments on her chassis; if you know what I mean."

"Oh yes; simply attend a meeting of your peers and you will find, somewhere in that mass of predominantly male jesters, one silver haired, but young, fair maiden, who will meet your requirements, Sir Lawrence of Arabia; uh, sir."

"Cool."

That dialogue never really took place, of course; but it sets the stage for what happens at the rental managers meeting in May of 1985. Also, I would never ask corporate to pimp itself out to find me a girl friend. They liked me, but that would've been ridiculous.

As the Phoenix Group slowly grew, the relationship I had with Jim Keene never quite became warm and fuzzy. His lack of knowledge of the rental business was becoming a bit of a problem, and it never seemed to fail that he'd say something not quite accurate in front of all the young, impressionable employees, at a dinner meeting or some such gathering. After the remark, the stunned employees would look my way for verification; and I'd be "waving it off" in much the same manner as a football referee signaling a penalty has been declined.

In perfecting the art of "waving off" an inaccurate comment made by a superior officer, one must stay properly positioned to execute the maneuver successfully. Assuming visibility is good for the rest of the team, I recommend the "behind the back wave" which is performed quickly, with low hand movement, while the offending party is looking at the team and you are positioned behind his back. If the offending party rotates his head to see what maneuver you may be executing, it will be too late to observe your action. After the initial "wave off" has been successfully executed, subsequent "wave offs" can be performed with less motion, utilizing the "head shake and eye roll combination".

Luckily, Jim and I gradually developed a tacit understanding that seemed to work; which basically allowed me to run the rental business in a way I saw fit, as long as I didn't screw anything up. As far as I can remember, I didn't screw anything up too badly.

By 1984, the Phoenix Group was becoming a pretty decent sized operation, and the original Mesa office frequently flirted with the top spot in the company on the old income and expense per unit analysis. Personally, I was raking in some pretty hefty commissions now, and as a show of my loyalty to Enterprise Leasing, I became one of Jim Keene's valued lease customers, looking sharp in a brand new ruby red '84 Porsche 944. I'm not sure if that deal had put Jim into double digits at that time, or if he was around eight or nine units leased. As I recall, he had his father-in-law in a car, as well as his neighbor, now me, plus a few other people. I think he might've made it to double digits then, which is really pathetic; let's face it.

Before I knew it, I was back in St Louis again, for another rental managers meeting. My rock star status remained intact with another brilliant monologue; and this time Kaufmann, quite the showman, had me going first. I did the old "Gee, I completely forgot to prepare a speech gag", which of course led to the "Luckily, I've got a transcript of last year's presentation gag"; whereupon I launched into the "Pedro Borbon-Manny Mota" routine; the crowd loved it, I proved I was no one hit wonder; and most of the other rental managers were now calling me "Pedro". I loved it; so many nicknames, not enough time.

Those were fun-loving times, really, the "glory years", which coincided with the Boss' song by that same name that came along right about then. The company was starting to grow like crazy, eclipsing the "100 office plateau" in May of 1983, which seemed like a very significant event, at the time.

However, before Enterprise became a colossal corporation, it was an exciting environment to inhabit; and it made recruiting new employees a relatively easy, and satisfying process. There was not only a lot of upward career potential for a bright and enthusiastic go-getter; there was a lot of fun going on, and some pretty good money to be made.

I was on the verge of experiencing first hand upward career potential like I never dreamed possible; and in the process being catapulted to a place I never really dreamed existed, at least for me.

My "glory years" were only beginning.

Chapter 13
The Tucson Debacle

I was just as happy as I could be in 1984. I would celebrate my tenth anniversary with the company in October, we now had five successful offices going, with plans to open our sixth in early '85 (which would act as our Airport branch), and I really enjoyed hanging out with my friends, who also happened to be my employees. We were one big happy family; it felt like old times again.

Then Tucson opened.

In one of Enterprise's worst blunders, the decision was made to take someone from outside the company, a retired Ford Motor executive by the name of Lu Slips train him in Phoenix for a couple of months, then send him on his merry way to finally open that smaller Arizona market.

Ironically, three years earlier, it was my responsibility to train Pam Taylor so she could open Tucson; and apparently corporate didn't learn its lesson from that disaster. Instead, they agree to take some old geezer who never spent a day in his life in a rental branch, plop him in my lap for a couple of months, and expect him to successfully run a new town.

The Tucson Experiment, Part II didn't work, either.

Lu Slips looked and sounded like a character actor from some really bad grade B gangster flick from the 1940s. I suppose Lu would've been in his mid 60s when he retired from the staid, highly structured and politically powered Ford Motor Company; he was completely bald; wore very nice suits, and when he spoke, it sounded like he was in a great deal of pain, but was trying to conceal that fact, because he didn't want anybody to worry about him. In the movies, he would've been gunned down very quickly; but he would've had maybe a line or two before his demise; something like, "You want I should ice that guy?"

Prior to his short-lived Enterprise career, Lu worked for Ford Motor Company for forty years or so, which in itself is a remarkable achievement; and upon his retirement, got Enterprise to agree to hire him for Tucson. It only made sense; after all, he was retiring to Tucson.

They should have let him retire in peace, or maybe iced that guy.

While Slips was going through the three-month training process which would still leave him completely unprepared for what would lie ahead, it was apparent to everybody in the Group that Lu had no clue, and would probably never get a clue on what to do to; and that was a fine how do you do; it's déjà vu all over again.

Unfortunately, I tried to convince the corporate brain trust to trust me on this, but to no avail. Like it or not, Lu Slips was going to open Tucson for Enterprise, end of discussion.

The fact of the matter was, I had three guys who were qualified to open Tucson; they were sufficiently experienced in the Enterprise way, they wanted to move up with the company, and they weren't on social security. It didn't matter; Lu was promised this deal and nothing; not even logic, could change that commitment.

As the Phoenix Group collectively shook its head in dismay, on April

1, 1984, a date that somehow seemed appropriate, Enterprise opened in Tucson. The boys at corporate thought it would be a good idea to have me go down there, to help get the new operation going; and that was a good idea. The only problem was I couldn't keep Tucson; I had to give it back and go back home.

With Tucson left in the incapable hands of Lu Slips and his unreliable assistant, a former employee with Enterprise in Southern California (I just can't for the life of me, remember his name), Tucson wrecked havoc for over two years before their annoying ineptitude ended. After the dust had settled, the Tucson operation was at the bottom of the list, month in and month out, in terms of their measurable performance; or lack thereof.

The Tucson Experiment, Part II had failed miserably, as Lu Slips definitely sank the Enterprise ship in the southeastern Arizona desert; but there would be rebirth a little over two years after the travesty began.

However, this happy Hollywood ending would take quite some time to materialize; there would be rough seas ahead, as our valiant effort to take Enterprise from the bottom of the heap would be met with great resistance from Lu Slips' incompetent cohort; a guy who quite arguably was the worst manager in the history of the company.

Chapter 14
My Enterprise Romance

Our sixth (and what would be my final) office in Phoenix opened in early 1985, which was officially dubbed our Airport branch; but it was essentially a trailer parked on a gravel lot on East Washington Street, serving those discriminating customers who demanded the very best; an inexpensive car, enthusiastic service, and dirty shoes.

Enterprise wasn't exactly a big time player in the lucrative air travel market in those days; in fact, I don't even think we were getting one tenth of one percent of that business, even by the end of the decade (By 2008, Enterprise became the largest car rental provider in the air travel market after gobbling up both Alamo and National a year earlier).

Back in 1985, as the City Manager of the fledgling Phoenix Group, I didn't care about any of the statistics; it just seemed to make sense to finally have an office that was reasonably close to the airport where we could not only handle those deplaning passengers, but take care of the local crack whore clientele as well.

Sure, it was a disgraceful looking office in a horrible neighborhood, but like so many other hideous looking low overhead Enterprise

Rent-a-Car branches scattered throughout the country, it made money, and that wasn't such a bad thing.

I recall sitting in my office, shortly after this ragtag trailer became profitable, and feeling very satisfied with things, almost like I'd completed a heroic mission; that I'd accomplished what I set out to do despite all the odds. Shortly before it was time to head to St Louis again for another rental managers meeting, I was thinking, "What now?"

Suddenly, Jim Loomer was promoted.

This came as quite a shock to everybody, not necessarily that he was promoted, but it was the locale that threw everyone for a loop; he was going to be the new City Manager of Columbia, South Carolina. Some of the Phoenix Group employees (I was one of them) actually got a road atlas to find out exactly where this remote southern city was located; and sure enough it was all the way out to the Atlantic Ocean, deep in the heart of Dixie.

After interviewing with Dick Rush, the good old boy from the '82 meeting who was so appalled by having some "leasing guy" come in and take over Phoenix; Dick later became General Manager of the soon to be very successful Southeast Group (which certainly helped pave the way for me to move up) and grabbed Loomer away from me, telling a somewhat surprised and overwhelmed Jim, "Hey, you're my buddy."

I was happy for Jim, who knew what he was doing; and Dick stayed true to his word, subsequently promoting "his buddy" to the larger Charlotte, North Carolina market; before putting in a good word to Doug Brown to get Jim the big promotion to General Manager of the newly formed Milwaukee Group, his old hometown, in the early '90s.

Jim later claimed he was relieved my Cardinals beat his Brewers in the 1982 World Series, so I wouldn't fire him; however, there's no evidence to support that theory; provided of course, he wouldn't gloat about it had the Cardinals fallen to the Brewers; that's just silly speculation; but it's a good thing my team won, anyway.

With Jim's promotion a cause for celebration; this was the first person I had ever hired in Arizona, and now he was moving up the ranks of this rapidly growing company; we headed to St Louis to attend the big rental manager's meeting. Those predominantly white male gatherings still looked like a Mormon convention in the mid '80s, although there were a sprinkling of women and minorities in the mix, but you had to look hard to find them.

One of the women in attendance at that predominantly white male jester filled meeting was a 28 year-old branch manager from Houston who ran a single office that had almost as many cars in service as the entire Phoenix Group. Prematurely gray when she was a teenager, yet strikingly beautiful and obviously much younger than the silver hair might suggest; Pamela Divine rose from a fairly mundane existence in Jackson, Mississippi where she was the youngest of three sisters, had an older and a younger brother, and a widowed mother; moved to Houston in 1980, interviewed with Andy Jansky, and was promptly hired.

Combining business savvy with southern charm and a "can do" attitude, Pam had a smile that captivated customers and employees alike, not to mention bumbling potential suitors, like me, as she confidently rose through the ranks with Enterprise.

Just a few months prior to this meeting, she interviewed for the position of City Manager of New Orleans, was offered the job by then General Manager, David White, and turned it down simply because she didn't like the guy. Apparently, White really liked Pam, but when he had the temerity to refer to her as his "silver fox", that tipped the scales against this typically cocky leasing guy. Not long afterwards, Larry Snow's replacement was given the boot as well; adding to the growing list of leasing guys who became fired General Managers.

Interestingly enough, the guy David White eventually hired used the

New Orleans promotion as a springboard to his career and would soon become a General Manager himself. Jack Talley was a likeable, all American clean-cut kid from Kansas City, originally, and almost made it as a professional baseball player. Whatever disappointment he may have felt by not quite making it as a ballplayer, was surely erased by the time he made it big as a General Manager with Enterprise.

Of course, Jack was very grateful to Pam for turning down New Orleans; and he also married a girl named "Jill", which I thought was so sweet.

When I laid eyes on Pam at the '85 meeting, I was determined to be as charming as possible and see where that would lead; I already knew her, but only slightly, from the previous year, partying into the wee hours the last night of our incarceration. However, the crowd was large and loud, and I didn't even get a chance to say anything at all charming or remotely witty to her.

This year would be different, I hoped, as I casually looked at her and slowly murmured, "Why Pamela, you look absolutely divine, this evening." She looked at me vacantly; and barely smiled; while striking a demeanor that seemed to suggest she'd been fed that line a thousand times before, waving me off like a sniveling groupie. Wait a minute; I was the rock star; or so I thought; suddenly, I didn't feel so good about myself.

The next day, as fate would have it, Pam was in my little group of managers that huddled after the big presentations were given; these were the notorious "break out" groups, and I think they were given that name because that's what everybody wanted to do while trapped in there. A handful of us had to lead some sort of discussion pertaining to some mundane part of the business, and I remember sitting there on that panel and looking glumly at the bored faces of young managers who weren't listening to a word we were saying.

Pam was sitting towards the back of the room smirking as she and her blonde friend, Denise, another Houston manager, were making fun of everything going on; which wasn't much. I felt like I had as much of a chance of making it with Pamela Gayle Divine as Pamela Sue Martin who everyone remembers played Nancy Drew on some sort of television program, back in the '70s. Pamela Anderson hadn't been "invented" yet, at least from a hot celebrity babe perspective; otherwise, I would've used her for this analogy; for sure.

As I settled in to the regular routine, I remember giving a fairly lame speech that year, by my standards, although the crowd response was decent; still, that was probably reputation carrying me. With Kaufmann thankfully ending the proceedings for that year, people jumped out of their seats like they were running for their lives, but in reality, they just wanted to change into something more comfortable and go out to get hammered somewhere, to celebrate their new found freedom.

I had no plans, in fact, I was slightly bummed out because I was unsuccessful in my attempt to rekindle any sort of romance with the beautiful Cindy Constantine, the woman I still adored from two years prior. She kind of blew me off the first night I was in town, and ordinarily, I would've seen her on that final night of captivity, but that just wasn't going to happen tonight, because I was kind of pissed.

While the rest of the managers scrambled out of that meeting room, knocking over chairs, and bumping into each other, acting like the place was on fire, I remained seated for a while, bemused by the scene.

I think Kaufmann and a few other people were still hanging around that now nearly abandoned hotel meeting room, when I finally decided to split. With the place nearly deserted, I realized it was pretty huge, and it had to be huge, to accommodate the ever growing number of meeting participants Enterprise would gather each year.

As I made my way back to my inconveniently situated hotel room, I glanced at my watch and realized the Cardinals game against the Astros might still be on, so wanting to catch the end I quickened my pace. By the time I made it to the room and turned on the television, it was the top of the ninth, as the Cardinals were losing, but attempting to rally; however, Darrel Porter finally flew out deep to right field to end it.

Being an insane Cardinals fan, every game was a big deal to me, and when Porter hit it, I thought it had a chance of leaving the yard, probably giving the Cards a thrilling come from behind victory; so I was screaming like a maniac, "Go! Go! Go!"

Afterwards I went into my post game ritual on those rare occasions the Redbirds lost in such heartbreaking fashion that year, "Fuck! Fuck! Fuck! That fucking Astrodome is ridiculous! How does anybody hit one out of that fucking place?" I'm sure the entire fifteenth floor could hear my ranting, but so be it.

Still fuming a little bit, after changing into some casual attire, my cool jeans and Nikes, I thought I'd head downstairs, and just do it; find some people to have a little fun with. In the old days, most of the guys played poker but as the crowd grew larger and more diverse, that tradition was falling by the wayside, at least as far as I was concerned.

As I was meandering along downstairs in no particular direction, I happened to run into my future ex-wife, Pamela Divine and a few of her pals, primarily from Houston. Pam's best friend, Denise, who was Pam's cohort in making fun of the break out group leaders earlier in the day, like me, for example; was a very cute girl but a bit shy, so she quietly hovered around Pam most of the time as much the way a devoted Collie, like Lassie would hover around her master, somehow getting a very important message delivered when it was crucial to the successful resolution of that plotline.

Pam looked at Lassie and said, "What is it girl? You think we should take Larry with us downtown to party like a rock star? But how would we get there, girl? What's that, girl; you think Van Black would give us a ride?"

Of course, that's what Pam and Lassie quickly engineered, hauling me off along with the rest of the entourage in the company car belonging to none other than Van Black, Enterprise's fun-loving meeting coordinator.

The next thing I knew, officer, I was squeezed in the front, middle seat of Van Black's Oldsmobile, with a contented Lassie seated to my right. Meanwhile, as the radio was blaring Rod Stewart singing "Maggie May", everybody in the car, including Lassie (but not Van) began to howl along with Rod, "I know I keep you amused, but I feel I'm being used."

I was having a great time already, while Van bravely smiled during our joyously off-key sing along; "I suppose I could collect my books and get on back to school, or steal my daddy's cue and make a living out of playing pool."

"Or find myself a rock and roll band that needs a helping hand."

I think Van was glad to give that howling bunch of managers a helping hand, all right; out of his nice, clean, company car, compliments of Enterprise Leasing, somewhere in the middle of St Louis. After we piled out, I looked back at Van who seemed a little out of sorts, but was still bravely smiling. I smiled right back at him, and gave him the quick, "thanks for the ride" salute; Van acknowledged my salute with a vague head motion, while his eyes comically rolled back into his head; and just like that, the car whisked away into the St Louis early May cool late night humidity, driven by the now frazzled Van Lear Black; truly a good guy.

Inside the bar were dozens of Enterprise revelers, already in mid season form. After many beers, a few forgettable games of pool, and a pathetic attempt to dance with my future sweetheart to Dire Straights' "Money for Nothing", we hailed a cab to head back to Enterprise land, after the bartenders told us we didn't have to go home but we couldn't stay there; actually, I think they said, "Get the fuck out of here, people."

As the cab driver somehow took the most round about route back to the hotel as possible; with both of us slightly intoxicated, Pam and I got a little serious with our discussion, as the topic soon became our good friend, the late Andy Jansky.

We both laughed and mostly cried as we reminisced about Andy and his fun-loving ways. Our eyes were still misty when we joined another group of revelers in one of the rooms. It was getting wild in there, and after a while, I looked at Pam, who was already looking at me, and we looked that look at each other, signifying the mating ritual had begun, in earnest; we slipped out of there without even being noticed by any possible, uh onlookers.

By this time, it must've been after 3 am, and we both fell for each other in a fairly wholesome PG-13 way. Apparently, there was some NC-17 rated stuff going on, as there always was at these gatherings, but it didn't involve the two of us. Dave Dieckmann thought it was us, and for years tried to pin the two naked bodies in some hotel whirlpool on us, but that urban legend was false; at least as far as any participation from Pam and I was concerned. I think Dave may have been a little jealous, but he would never admit it.

The rest of the summer was spent in a long distance, whirlpool, uh whirlwind, romance. I married my second wife in Houston on August 24, 1985; and in the process, Houston probably lost its best rental manager, and I found the woman who would be the mother of my two wonderful children; Justin and Taryn, who are both young adults now and don't think it's cool to read this book, but maybe they really think it's cool deep down inside.

Although our marriage didn't work out, long term, Pam and I had some wonderful times together, and I don't think either one of us would've changed a thing.

Chapter 15
Hitting The Career Jackpot

nside of a year after tying the knot with Pam, and just a little over five years after first opening the Phoenix Group, I got the call from the three head-honchos at corporate that began, "Larry, this is Doug Brown, and on the speaker phone with me is Andy Taylor and Don Ross."

I figured they were going to offer me a promotion, and this time I was going to take it, no matter where it would station me. Hell, if they offered me Seattle again, I'd say, "I love rain, cooler weather, and I hear there's a new sound on the horizon that will change the face of rock forever; grunge rock; so let's have another cup of Starbucks and rock!"

They didn't offer me Seattle.

Aside from polite tidbits of conversation from Andy and Don, Doug did most of the talking and as his words zipped right along, I only had time to give a quick, "Uh-huh", every now and then just to let him know I was following every word of his manic conversation as if my life depended on it.

This was the guy who interviewed me twelve years ago; although I don't recall too much of what he was telling me back then, since I was so preoccupied with just trying to land a job; and now, this same guy was going to offer me something that would pay me a bit more than the $650 a month that lured me into working for this company to begin with.

Finally, after a brief discussion of the corporate philosophy that now enabled ordinary rental guys like me the opportunity to become a General Manager, like Dave Willey (1984) and Dick Rush (1985) before me; my territory would be comprised of a string of cities that were considered "too small" individually to form a viable Group, but when clustered together, they should work out just fine; hopefully.

These types of Groups had a special name; the "Mid-Cities" Groups, which guys like Dave Willey thought sounded demeaning, as if to say "Since you can't handle a regular sized city with a leasing operation, we'll let you have these little cities where we would never even think about opening a leasing operation, which in turn, now qualifies you, a daily reptile veteran, the chance to become a real, live General Manager."

I could see his point; even though we were General Managers, it was almost like the company had to put an asterisk by the title, since leasing would be out of the picture. Big deal, I figured we'd do okay just renting them daily reptiles.

Looking back on it, I suppose I would've made "history" had I accepted the Seattle offer; after all, it was a fairly large market, and no asterisks would've been required, but I'm still glad I got the Mid-Cities West Group anyway.

The conversation seemed to be going on for a very long time, before Doug finally cut to the chase. Looking back on it, apparently Doug was just making some of this stuff up as he went along, which really seems strange, since Andy and Don were on the phone, as well.

He began; "Larry, the deal we've been kicking around here would be called the West Group. Now, if you've got a pen (of course I did),

I'll give you the cities we think would fit into this new operation." He paused for a moment then bombarded me with "Tucson, Las Vegas, Albuquerque, El Paso, Reno, Salt Lake City, and Sacramento." That was seven cities in less than seven seconds. I wasn't sure, but that sounded like some sort of record to me; my head sure was spinning, as if I made the actual trips to those cities as they were being named; I felt like I was in a Huey Lewis video, while my heart of rock and roll was really beating now, in Phoenix.

As I'm scribbling these cities down, the conversation on the other end has paused, now waiting for me to say something of substance. Just as I finished scribbling "Sacramento", I remark brilliantly, " Guys, this sure sounds great. Uh."

They knew I was flabbergasted, so rather than waste any more of their time, Doug suggested he call back tomorrow, to allow time to regroup. After carefully checking my day planner, I said I could fit him in, any time; any time he wanted to call was fine with me. He laughed the raspy Doug Brown laugh, and said, "Okay, Underdog; I'll talk to you tomorrow."

After hanging up the phone, I remained dumbfounded for quite some time; almost too shocked to be happy, but nervously anticipating a challenging and potentially lucrative future; I was thinking to myself, "Is this really happening?"

The next day, as promised, Doug called me back without Andy and Don chirping in; who needed them, anyway? After exchanging pleasantries, Doug delivered a quick jab, which caught me off guard, to say the least. Doug had a way of delivering bad news to make you think it wasn't so bad at all, as he casually said, "Oh, Larry, after kicking around the list of cities that would be included in the West Group, we thought about it some more, and made a few changes."

"Oh, yeah?" When Doug said he wanted to regroup, he literally meant, "re-Group".

"Yeah. Here's the new deal; instead of Salt Lake City and

Sacramento, we're replacing that with Fresno and Bakersfield. We feel the new bundle of cities ties in better, and will be more manageable than that first deal that we kind of thought about yesterday."

Oh really? It was more manageable all right, because it was a lot smaller. I just lost about three million unmanageable people out of my newly bundled Group, and I hadn't even started yet. There was no way to win by objecting to the new configuration, so I quickly agreed, before I lost Las Vegas.

The fact that the three top guys in the company didn't quite have everything figured out, except for the fact that they wanted to make me a General Manager, exemplifies the good old fashioned "fly by the seat of your pants" business plan that entrepreneurial companies put together. As far as I was concerned, that way of doing business suited me just fine; it seemed to me that the people who were most successful in the company weren't afraid to make a few mistakes along the way; they always seemed to have a back up plan ready to go, and eventually, things usually worked out just fine.

This time around, the guaranty was doubled, to $48,000 for the first year, with slight increases over the next couple of years. Had I stayed in Phoenix that first year, I would've made twice that, but while my replacement started driving a Corvette and had a nice Rolex, I just focused on my goal; which was to get off the guaranty and on the normal pay plan within three years.

The commission was, as it turned out, absolutely ridiculous, but I had to take it---15% of net profit; and I must say, that amounted to one hell of a lot of money during my profitable career; more money than I ever dreamed possible; or Enterprise ever dreamed possible, for that matter; but that was the story for those fortunate souls on the original pay plan; assuming they made their Group a profitable enterprise for Enterprise.

Then Doug tempered my elation with a bit of a warning about Fresno and Bakersfield. "Larry, there's a very strong competitor in the San

Joaquin Valley; a family owned company called 'Standard Rent-a-Car'. When you open up there, prepare for war. They're as tough as any company we've ever seen. You might want to call Stan Mann (Doug's right hand man at corporate) since he can tell you a lot about them; and call Bill Hole (Southern California Group), and Lenny Alma (San Francisco Group); they'll fill you in. Good luck!"

So now, in addition to losing three million people, they're being replaced with one million people who won't want to rent from us. Fuck it. I always liked a good challenge.

I'd finally made the big time. I'd just received my fourth promotion with Enterprise, and like the three others previously, I didn't even have to interview for it to get it.

I didn't really know what to expect but I figured things would fall into place. Dick Jansen had moved from Phoenix to Tucson just a few weeks prior, and would eventually straighten that mess out. Everything else was an unknown quantity, but I wasn't worried. I was optimistic, but even in my wildest dreams I never would have predicted the size and scope that would define the West Group within a decade.

I also never would have predicted the challenges that would be facing me in dealing with the once friendly corporate hierarchy within the next decade.

After the dust had settled fourteen years later, the West Group would become the fifth most profitable rental operation in the entire company, trailing only Southern California, New York, San Francisco, and Chicago; and I would be retiring.

Chapter 16
Striving For Credibility

On August 1, 1986, my first act as General Manager was to piss Jim Keene off. I wasn't trying to piss him off, but that's what happened anyway when Christy Reed, a clerical type person, deserted Jim to come work for me as my administrative assistant, which was a bit of a promotion for her.

I was able to lure Christy away, not only because I'm so charming, but I had planned to establish the new administrative office in Phoenix, since it was pretty much smack dab in the middle of my massive territory, was the hub for America West Airlines, so getting out to the cities in the Group was an easy process. Had I moved up to Las Vegas, I would've had to find another administrative assistant; her husband had a good job in Phoenix, had commitments with the Arizona Air National Guard to fulfill, so that was that. Years later, when we finally made the move to Lost Wages, Christy said "see you later" and bolted back over to the Phoenix Group, where she's still gainfully employed to this day.

A few weeks prior to Christy's transfer to my new Group, Keene lost one of his best branch managers, as Dick Jansen slid down to Tucson to become the first legitimate City Manager that town so desperately needed, but that was before I got promoted. I got lucky and inherited Dick.

When I left the Phoenix Group, there were a number of my former employees who also wanted to transfer to Uncle Larry's new Group; Jim vehemently objected, and got corporate involved in the dispute.

I don't blame him; but I had to get some talent from somewhere and Phoenix seemed to be a good place to get the ball rolling; so I grabbed Tom Tobin to start up the new Las Vegas operation, and along with Tom came a fellow named Les who would be Tom's assistant.

After that, a moratorium was placed on any more of my evil poaching for another year; and that seemed reasonable. Still, the die was cast; Phoenix would carry on a tradition of despising the West Group for as long as I was its General Manager. Whatever happened to teamwork? I still loved Phoenix.

Aside from all that nonsense, my biggest challenge was the lack of credibility this new fangled West Group would experience in the early going. Nobody in the company, and I mean nobody, thought the Wild, Wild West had much of a chance of becoming the giant it would eventually become. On the contrary, there were many who believed it would suck; because at the time we had only a horrible track record; but that was based on what Lu Slips' Tucson had done up to that point, which of course, was suck, while sinking to the bottom of the Enterprise ocean.

In the meantime, I'm trying to bring on board somebody adventurous enough to be my Business Manager, to no avail. I even had one guy who worked at corporate, and was a lock to get the job, but he got cold feet and didn't accept my offer; then he sort of left the company altogether, shortly thereafter. That was weird.

Finally, a legitimate candidate surfaced, from the Atlanta Group; a young man by the name of Dave Vogt who at twenty-six years, looked and sounded like he was about half that age. Dave and his bitchy wife, Cheri, who would later divorce Dave, agreed to move to

Phoenix, so the only real candidate for the job is now on board. That would be the ongoing theme as the West Group looked to fill several key spots.

With Tucson heading in the right, albeit bumpy, direction; the task of determining a "short list" of viable candidates for the new City Manager positions is ready to begin. The short list in Las Vegas includes Tom Tobin, and no one else because I knew that's where I wanted him to go, and fortunately, he agreed.

The Albuquerque short list included a short guy from Dallas, Scott Kendrick, and no one else. Yes, he was the only legitimate candidate who was willing to go there. Another guy from Southern California got cold feet on the deal, and then along came Scott who worked out quite well for me during my tenure as General Manager; first in Albuquerque, then years later in Las Vegas. When I retired, Scott got farmed out to Sacramento, and then was later put out to pasture there.

Meanwhile, back in Tucson, the carnage left by Lu Slips is slowly fading away, but Jansen is facing serious opposition from the guy that Lu dragged with him to Tucson, from Southern California, when Tucson first opened for business. This goofball was quite possibly the worst manager in the history of Enterprise, as his office always seemed to be at the absolute bottom of the list, month in and month out. On top of that, he was an asshole to his employees and customers alike, was dishonest, and lazy. When Dick gave him his annual review, it was right on the money, as his performance was ranked about as low as you can go in just about every measurable category.

When we caught him doing a bunch of dishonest stuff, we fired his ass. Naturally, he sued for wrongful termination, and proving that it's difficult for big companies (or even small, as we were then) to ever win cases of this nature, he walked away with a tidy six-figure sum. The jury's shocking decision is another example of common sense in America taking a leave of absence. Generally speaking, the legal system in this country is a joke; and that's no joke.

Even though we never should've lost that case, it was worth it to pay the money to have this cancer go away. After we got rid of him, Tucson gradually began rising towards the upper echelon of the company in all measurable categories. We don't think that was a coincidence.

El Paso was the next to open, in the spring of 1987. Dallas supplied us with another City Manager, and again, the decision was made very easily since Greg Toast was the only person on the short list, since he was the only person in the entire company willing to get on that short list. Luckily, he accepted the position, in short order.

Greg was a likeable, but not particularly strong rental guy; he just wasn't aggressive enough to post good numbers, and he seemed overwhelmed most of the time. A few years later, he was given the chance to do something noteworthy in Albuquerque, and it never really materialized. He was an honest, hard working individual, but he was working in the wrong capacity with the company. When he made the switch to the "operations" side of the business, things started clicking for him. When I retired, he transferred to Chicago, where he was doing quite well, the last I heard.

In early 1988, Reno opened, and with the moratorium lifted on snagging Phoenix employees, I recruited Ed Player, who I hired back in '82, after the Pam Taylor firing; and he accepted my offer to become City Manager in Northern Nevada. Steady Eddie made the short list a party of one, accepted the job, and off to Reno he went.

Ed was a pretty big guy, and before hooking on with Enterprise, was a pitcher in the San Francisco Giants organization, setting numerous minor league records with the Phoenix Giants, primarily as a reliever. Ed never quite made it all the way, although he was up for a cup of coffee for San Francisco in the late '70s; he lost his control, then eventually his pitching job.

He came to Enterprise with kind of a "woe is me" attitude, probably because of all the grief he went through by not only losing his baseball job, but also having to deal with a wife who never seemed pleased about anything. In the early '90s, after getting promoted outside of the Group, he ran into trouble dealing with his new bosses, and was forced out of his job in Spokane, Washington, complaining about everything on the way out.

The most challenging of all the markets, and in many respects, the most fascinating, was the Fresno-Bakersfield operation, which opened up just before Reno, in late '87. I was forewarned that this would be a very tough market to break into, since Standard Rent-a-Car virtually owned that market. In choosing a City Manager for this operation, I wanted somebody with a proven track record in sales, and most of all, somebody who was fearless.

What I got was Brian Meade, from Southern California who seemed to be the ideal candidate for this position; he made the one-person short list, and that was that. He was aggressive, very dynamic, and self-assured. What I didn't know was that he came with a lot of baggage, and things got very volatile in the San Joaquin Valley in a hurry, and it had nothing to do with our battle with Standard Rent-a-Car.

Within only a few months, the guy who seemed ideal for the job was causing a mutiny amongst his employees, and I would soon have my hands full dealing with the backlash.

Chapter 17
Big Trouble In Little Fresno

One of my favorite Enterprise Groups was the massive Southern California Group, which on the Enterprise numerical scale was better known as "Group 32". The reason I liked that Group so much is they farmed out a lot of people to the West Group (we were "Group 54") and I certainly appreciated that.

That didn't mean the two Groups always saw eye to eye on things; in fact, we had a few skirmishes over the years, but the biggest disagreement I had with then General Manager of Group 32, Bill Hole, was over the guy he dished on us to run Fresno, the aforementioned Brian Meade.

When I tried to find candidates to fill the Fresno City Manager position, Brian very enthusiastically put his name in the hat. I had known Brian for a few years, just from our conversations at the managers meetings in St Louis. I really liked the guy; he had a terrific sense of humor, and he really seemed to be on top of his game, from a business perspective. It's hard to believe, but Brian, like all the other guys I hired before him, was the only candidate for that particular opening, therefore making a clean sweep of the one candidate short list.

Naturally, I was hoping to get a glowing recommendation from Bill and the other head-honcho in Group 32, Ira Robb.

They both concurred that Brian was a great pick for Fresno, although Ira demurred slightly, saying, "Larry, from time to time you've got to slow him down a little; he gets really worked up sometimes." Hell, as far as I was concerned, I'd rather have somebody that gets a little worked up than somebody who doesn't. Sure, I could see Brian was the excitable type, but good leaders and good marketers should lean in that direction; so as far as I was concerned, Ira's passing comment meant little to me as I was getting ready to wage war with the dreaded Standard Rent-a-Car.

When Brian stormed into Fresno, he did so with a tremendous amount of enthusiasm, and the two people he brought on board with him from Group 32, seemed to share his same passion for the business. It seemed that as we launched our quest, everybody was on the same page, and everybody was prepared for war.

The night Tom Lawless homered off Frank Viola to give the Cardinals a thrilling win over the Minnesota Twins in the '87 World Series; I thought anything was possible, as Brian and his little Enterprise entourage cheered for my team over dinner and drinks at Stuart Anderson's Black Angus, although I'm sure none of them really gave a shit. That didn't matter to me; these kids seemed great, they sucked up in a way that didn't come across as overbearing, and I thought, "Why shouldn't we be successful in Fresno? We're doing it everywhere else."

Symbolically, St Louis lost that World Series to those Homer Hanky Twins, and the West Group was losing its battle with Standard Rent-a-Car, primarily from internal strife within our once close-knit family of Fresno employees.

During those difficult early months, it was a slow and painful process to grab any business from the competition; although apparently, the folks at Standard were aware of every move we made, and did everything in their power to thwart our efforts. Fresno lost a lot of money, from the onset, but we expected that; this was going to be a very long battle, and ultimately, one we'd win several years down the road; however, for now, it was getting a little frustrating, and it was becoming apparent that Brian's abrasive approach to marketing was backfiring, more than just a little bit.

By May of '88, the two employees that Brian brought up with him from Southern California, expressed concern with me how Brian was handling certain issues dealing with the cash box, and became suspicious that he was dipping into the kitty for items that weren't business related.

I flew to Fresno to talk to Brian, and after getting Doug Brown and Stan Mann involved (Doug's right hand man, and prior to that Andy Jansky's former assistant at the South County office in St Louis), it was decided to have Brian fly to St Louis to be interrogated at length about anything even remotely related to cash box issues, by both Doug and Stan. By this time, now all the Fresno employees have banded together in their opposition to Brian, because none of them felt they could place their trust in Brian's hands.

Meanwhile, in St Louis, after extensive interrogation by Doug Brown and Stan Mann, Brian is exonerated of any wrong doing, and is on his way back to Fresno thinking everything's going to be back to normal. Upon his arrival, I meet with him and explain to him the situation with all his employees; I believe there were about a dozen or so. I just lay it on the table, saying, "Brian, we've got to get you out of Fresno. If you stay, we won't have any employees, so we're going to have to move you. I'll start making some phone calls right away, because there's no way you're going to be able to stay here."

I felt that as far as Brian was concerned, he should be happy he wasn't getting fired. Not many people get called to corporate to be interrogated about some possible malfeasance, and continue their career. Within a couple of days, I found a new home for Brian, in South Florida, and off he went.

The Fresno employees were shocked by all this, but I explained to them the situation; that Brian answered all the questions in a manner that got him off the hook; so right or wrong, that's the way it was, so let's get on with renting cars again.

Bill Hole was livid; and when I heard that, from Stan Mann, I called Bill to confront him on the issue. I said, "Bill how in the world did you expect me to fire Brian when he went through an extensive interrogation process at corporate, and passed it with flying colors?" Bill then went off on a tangent about how Brian had been in trouble like this before in Southern California. "Really? How come there's absolutely nothing in his personnel file about that? And how come neither you nor Ira mentioned a word of any of that to me when I was taking him off your hands?"

That was that; Bill was still pissed, and I was irritated that he'd be giving me shit about something that wasn't even documented in his file previously; aside from the fact that Brian got the "good housekeeping seal of approval" from Doug Brown. Nobody was really happy about the way the whole thing played out; but that's business.

As a footnote to this, within a year or so, Brian got promoted to the City Manager position in the newly formed Seattle Group. His General Manager was my old assistant manager at the Clayton office, Rick Goode, the guy notorious for cocking his right eyebrow when saying just about anything. Rick would later ax Brian before getting the ax himself. Before they got axed, they axed Ed Player, the guy who opened Reno for me.

If it sounds like a lot of people get axed at Enterprise, that's not necessarily true, but this is big business, baby; and in the case of Seattle, that operation became a black hole right from the beginning.

Now, I felt fortunate I stayed in Phoenix for a while longer.

Chapter 18
Successfully Achieving Credibility

As I said previously, I liked Group 32. In the wake of the Fresno debacle, they supplied us with another City Manager for Fresno, and this one was a keeper. Ira Robb personally called me to tell me about his guy, Robert Ward who not only consistently posted strong numbers; he had no skeletons in his closet. Done deal.

Robert was the perfect manager for the slower paced, laid back Fresno market, and his leadership helped get that operation finally rolling. He was familiar with all the small towns lined up and down the San Joaquin Valley, and he aggressively opened branches in those towns. When he told me little old Porterville was going to be a "gold mine", he was right.

Robert's successful stay in Fresno ran until 1992, when he got promoted to a General Manager's position of the newly formed Mountain Group. He moved up somewhere in the mountains and now kills large animals in addition to renting cars. He did a wonderful job in Fresno, and his replacement, Brett Todd, who of course came to us from Group 32, picked up right where Robert left off.

Those two guys, along with the Sacramento and San Francisco

Groups refusing to give an inch in our united alliance against Standard, were the catalysts behind the acquisition of that once ferocious competitor in 1996; a deal that was like a Clint Eastwood western, "good, bad, and ugly". I'll discuss that fiasco later.

Las Vegas was performing sensationally, and in the fall of 1990, after only four years as City Manager, Tom Tobin was promoted to a General Manager's position in Central Pennsylvania. Tom only opened three offices in Las Vegas; one on the east side of town in a little strip center, one on the west side of town in a little strip center, and one close to the airport, in a facility Enterprise still uses today. Those first two offices ranked number one and two, in the company for what were considered "new branches", and looking good on paper certainly worked for Tom. Brown loved him, and that was all there was to it.

Ira Robb did it again, sending me Tony Moist for the vacant City Manager's position in Las Vegas. Tony, who is maybe 5'6"--- was dubbed by Ira as "a good little business man", and he was. I liked Tony, but ending a phone conversation was difficult with him; he never really said anything, yet he never wanted to hang up. It was strange, but as the conversation would tail off and you were about ready to say "goodbye", Tony would mumble something that would somehow keep it going for another half hour or so. I'm glad I don't have to talk to him on the phone anymore.

Then there was Ed Player. Ed was taking a somewhat unusual step by taking on the City Manager position in Spokane. He was already City Manager in Reno, but he was restless; so off to a new Group he went, and unfortunately, things didn't work out well for him. He'd bitterly complain about things that were uncontrollable, so complaining only painted him as a malcontent; but I suppose he was. He didn't last long in Spokane, and it's unfortunate, because he could've been a stellar performer, but he lacked the positive energy and focus.

With Ed's departure from Reno, I placed Steve Tanner in that vacant spot, moving him over from Bakersfield. I overvalued Steve's abilities, and it was one of the biggest mistakes I would make. I erroneously pegged Steve as a real go-getter and a guy that could take that operation to greater heights. In reality, he was a guy who never really felt comfortable running that operation, nor driving any sort of marketing plan to make Reno a top-notch city. He seemed to lack focus and was easily distracted by mundane things that he'd do instead of delegate it to a lot attendant or somebody along those lines.

I really liked Steve, and I suppose that was where I went astray with him. I assumed he would be able to handle things that seemed very simple but frequently, that just wasn't the case; sometimes I'd wonder if he had any common sense at all. Reno didn't collapse while Steve was in charge; but it didn't thrive the way it should have.

With Tom Tobin's promotion up and out of the Group, Dick Jansen and Tony Moist, two guys who would become very close friends, as their careers almost seemed to parallel one another's emerged as the leaders among the City Managers.

Dick was one of those guys who everybody seemed to like, and he always seemed to be in the right place to get a free lunch or a free round of golf. He was a smooth hustler and I considered him a friend during his time in Phoenix and later Tucson. In the '80s he was deliberately and flagrantly politically incorrect. Although that would be a joking façade, it still created problems in managing his employees. He had somewhat of a short temper and he'd hold a grudge for months over some petty issue, if things didn't go his way. He had little patience for new employees who didn't interact with him in the way he preferred and would often ridicule those people behind their back.

However, for the most part, Dick was your biggest supporter if you showed you cared about whatever he cared about, and if you worked hard to achieve good results. If you made it into his inner circle, you'd be invited to tag along on his frequent golf outings with his buddies from State Farm or various dealerships around town. It was definitely good for business, but I think most importantly, as far as

Dick was concerned, it was very good for him.

Whatever magic he worked, it got him promoted to a General Manager's position in the mid '90s, first in Austin, Texas, and years later, in Atlanta, where he finally ran into a corporate buzz saw who didn't think the Jansen way was necessarily the best way.

Tony Moist, who ran Las Vegas in the early '90s, was very analytical and thoughtful, and did some wonderful things there until he apparently got sick of the lifestyle; and for some reason wanted to work at the corporate office. Tony would probably keep working for Enterprise forever, if they'd let him. I think he likes the safety and security of working for a huge corporation, and is working very hard to please the head-honchos. So far, he's been smart enough to pull it off. I certainly had no complaints during his brief stint with me. At the time of this writing, Tony is the General Manager of my original old stomping grounds, the St Louis Group, making him the shortest General Manager in St Louis Group history.

About two and a half years after I left the Phoenix Group, Jim Keene finally got the ax.

I think his lack of knowledge about the rental business may have caught up with him, or it may have been his lack of productivity on the leasing side of the business. Whatever the root cause for his exit from the company, it was clear the Phoenix Group was underperforming.

I heard there were some morale issues, and it's likely that Steve Gustav, the City Manager who replaced me, was not as decisive on some issues as he probably should've been; and as a result, Keene's weaknesses became even more glaring. Steve was fired not long afterwards, as a new management team tried to spark the Group to better performance.

It didn't work. Phoenix languished until late 2003, when they brought Tom Tobin back to the Group where it all began twenty years earlier for him. In 2006, the Phoenix Group finally got the

President's Award they had been waiting for since the inception of those awards in 1987; although I think now they're called a Chairman's Award or something. Whatever.

At the 1990 Fall Officers Meeting, which was held in Phoenix, two General Managers were promoted from Vice President to President of their subsidiaries: Dick Rush and Ed McCarty, who ran the Washington, DC Group. Both guys were among my favorites as far as Officers go, and I was excited for both of them when the announcement was made on the evening the President's Awards were doled out. I was also anticipating perhaps the following year, joining them in that elite club; I'd just won a second consecutive award, was still in favor with corporate, so yes, I felt like I was on the threshold.

That night, happily clutching my President's Award, I danced like Fred Astaire when the band started playing, and grinning like I was in a movie where all the dancers have a perpetual smile on their faces. My smile was genuine, and looking back on it, that was probably the happiest moment of my Enterprise business life.

I felt confident that I'd be getting that bump up to the Presidential suite by the next Fall Officers Meeting, and that tremendous feeling of accomplishment to me, was the equivalent of winning a Super Bowl or World Series.

If I was ever on the threshold, I definitely fell off it in early 1991, less than three months after that meeting; and I'd have nobody else to blame but myself. I had fallen out of favor, and there really was no getting it back.

Chapter 19

An Ominous Beginning To A New Decade

Sometime during the course of 1990, John Wilmer, who was the Phoenix Group's Remarketing Manager (responsible for selling cars on a wholesale basis) asked for, and received permission from Phoenix General Manager, Tom McHale, to join the slightly larger West Group, in the same capacity.

That move may have given me a false sense of security that all would be right in the world of remarketing in the West Group, forever. Wrong.

Ironically, just months after John joins our team, we screw up a huge transaction to some low-life criminal asshole from Utah by the name of Bob Steele. This con artist "bought" about twenty some odd cars from us in Reno, wrote a bunch of bad checks to us, and not only took delivery of the cars, our people in Reno went ahead and gave this bastard the fucking titles to the cars. We never tracked Bob Steele down, but more than likely, a low-life like that is dead now.

I'm pretty sure the corporate hierarchy wanted me to fire John Wilmer in the aftermath of this bungled transaction; and they probably expected it; but there were so many things that went wrong at so many different levels, that I didn't feel it was appropriate to take the easy way out by simply firing John and calling it a day.

Our "point person" in Reno was none other than Steve Tanner's dad, an amiable retiree who offered to help us out in moving some of our old cars that had been taken out of service.

John specifically told him, "Make sure you don't give him the titles to the cars until the checks clear." He must've heard, "Make sure you give him the titles to the cars because we want to get burned when the checks don't clear."

Dave Vogt, my baby-faced Business Manager, Wilmer and I decided to reimburse the company for one half of the loss out of our own pockets; so the company only got burned for $30,000 and we ate the rest; that seemed fair; but I knew going forward that my relationship with corporate would be damaged, possibly irrevocably; that Vogt and Wilmer would fall out of favor as well.

This was a major screw up that would forever tarnish the image of the Group; and as its General Manager, I am ultimately accountable for its consequences.

Vogt was widely regarded on the lower echelon of Business Managers before this mess, and was now totally vilified by the accounting gurus at corporate; there would be no saving his career; by the end of '96, he'd be gone. Wilmer survived to transfer to corporate after my retirement, working for a guy, Tim Welsh, who in the late '90s, was the guy I reported to at corporate, and once lambasted me for not getting rid of John because he was "only average" as a Group Remarketing Manager.

Other than the Fiasco Heard 'Round the Enterprise World, the West Group had a decent fiscal year for '91, and may have been in line to receive a President's Award at the Fall Officers Meeting at Amelia Island, in Florida. I knew there was no way in hell that would happen and I also knew the possibility of me ever getting promoted to President of my subsidiary anytime soon, was about as slim as Bob Steele paying us that sixty grand.

Chapter 20

Under The Corporate Microscope

The disappointment of realizing my career would probably stagnate; that I would get no higher than "Vice President" in the Enterprise system; was mollified by my ever increasing annual income. My goal each year was simply to survive another year.

As my annual income soared past the one million dollar plateau in the early '90s, it was nice to be rich, but it was getting more difficult to find peace of mind. In an effort to placate Pam, who was becoming increasingly frustrated with being the stay-at-home mom with two small kids, while I was frequently off on business trips, I made her an offer she gladly accepted.

"Let's move into our dream house, and get you a live-in nanny to help with the kids."

That seemed like such a simple solution, and Pam wholeheartedly agreed, but a funny thing happened on the way to the dream house. We separated in early '95 about a year after we bought the big mansion in Paradise Valley.

The mansion, which was built in the early '70s, needed a complete overhaul, which not only cost hundreds of thousands of dollars, but also took many, many months to complete. About four months after we separated, Pam and the kids moved into the beautiful dream house, and I was living down the street.

The reasons couples split up are usually complex, but it usually boils down to one simple explanation; they don't get along. Realizing we would never get along, we decided to go our separate ways, and my peace of mind was restored, at least temporarily.

Ironically, although I ultimately restored peace of mind in my personal life by taking what many perceive to be a socially unacceptable action (especially at Enterprise); my relationship with the corporate brain trust, which had always been cordial and appropriately autonomous; now was on the verge becoming something quite tumultuous and anything but cordial.

Over the years, the company went from having a fairly loose corporate structure to one that became very defined. Drones, known as Corporate Vice Presidents, came along to inform and/or placate the corporate big wigs by micro-managing the General Managers in the field. Any flaw in a Group's performance, real or imagined, became dissected until the problem was either resolved or accepted as an indigenous part of that Group, like it or not.

At times, the Corporate Vice Presidents would confer with the big wigs and determine that the root cause of the problem being dissected was the result of deficient action by the General Manager under the microscope. In those cases, the General Manager was usually sent packing and a replacement was quickly brought in; this in turn created "opportunity" for the employees in the trenches to move up a notch, if they met the necessary requirements.

Quite often, getting rid of a General Manager also created the "opportunity" for the corporation to save money by bringing in a lower commissioned replacement, and/or by carving up the former General Manager's Group and giving the sliced up portions to other Groups, usually which had General Managers already in place with a significantly lower pay plan, or creating new Groups, and in turn promoting new General Managers, again in most cases, with significantly lower pay plans.

That was the scenario I was trying to avoid in the mid '90s, when I received a visit from my new Corporate Vice President, Ernie Badger. I had known Ernie for quite a long time; the relationship was cordial, but never close. In recent years, we had gotten a little closer through mutual friends that we associated with at the Fall Officers Meetings, which also included spouses; Pam and Ernie's wife Marie seemed to hit it off, and Ernie seemed to enjoy Pam's company as well.

After the 1992 meeting, which was held in San Francisco, a bunch of us went down to the Monterey Peninsula afterwards, primarily to experience the tremendous golf, with the featured attraction being the legendary Pebble Beach Golf Links. Playing that course for the first time had me so rattled I nearly whiffed my opening tee shot, which traveled just far enough to fall off the tee. It was by far the most embarrassing moment of my life.

Playing the rest of the day with Ernie in my foursome and overanalyzing every possible shot he was faced with didn't help my morale. Ernie's caddy, a weather beaten veteran of toting bags for hacks and pros alike, very quickly got tired of this particular pompous hack trying to act like the US Open was at stake, and would frequently implore, "Just hit it, for crying out loud!"

Ernie never really changed his frustratingly painstaking approach to the round, which must have tallied at least a hundred strokes by the time he tapped in his one footer on number 18 for another double bogey. As the round mercifully ended his poor caddy could hardly wait to get out of there, presumably to the nearest watering hole where a few Jack Daniels might ease the memory of a very long five hours of torture.

When Enterprise "Leasing" became "Fleet Services", a couple of years after that '92 golf trip, the focus was shifted away from the "individual" lease customer to the "fleet" lease customer; typically companies that lease twenty cars or so. Previously, there was just one division of the company called "Enterprise Fleet Services", and that was the division Ernie ran. Suddenly, Ernie was out of a job, but not for long. The man who never spent a day in his life behind a rental counter was made a Corporate Vice President; but he knew leasing, so that made sense.

Now the task at hand was to assign some Groups to Ernie, so he could practice his craft. He was assigned all of the Texas Groups, Atlanta, Phoenix; and of course, the West Group.

At first, he kept his distance and it seemed like we'd get along just fine and I'd keep my peace of mind; but that was just a temporary respite.

Ernie then decided to make a Group visit, sometime around late April 1995. After exchanging the obligatory business pleasantries in the Arizona warmth, as I picked him up from the airport, he seemed a little tired from the extensive amount of travel he had subjected himself to, making the rounds of many of the cities throughout the Group, accompanied by either Tucson-based Dick Jansen or Las Vegas-based Scott Kendrick; depending on the portion of the Group he happened to be visiting. After mentioning some favorable comments and some not so favorable comments, he preferred to go into more detail the next day, so the conversation shifted to the home life.

"So, how's Pam?" Ernie's blank expression seemed to suggest he was already anticipating my bland reply, "Oh, she's fine." I think he was then going to say something like, "Well, tell her I said, 'Hello.'"

Instead, I told him we were separated. The look on his face said everything to me. His demeanor for the rest of the trip seemed to reflect his disapproval over this situation. It was apparent that he perceived me to be the bad guy in our separation, which of course was none of his business at all; but he made it his business.

The next day, as I was giving him a ride to the airport, he was lecturing me about something mundane, and I tried my best to look like it was a very good idea, and that I'd implement it right away, after careful review and consideration. He then glared at me and sternly said, "You know, Underwood; you don't give a damn about what we at corporate think!" I did a double take; I thought at first he was just giving me some good-natured kidding. He continued to glare. I realized he was serious; but as I defended the way I conduct business, I could see it wasn't what he wanted to hear.

As he got out of the car at the TWA terminal, grabbed his briefcase and carry-on bag, and gave me the obligatory final wave, I knew this was going to be a difficult situation to handle.

Chapter 21

Being Dissected Under The Miscroscope

I wasn't sure how long Ernie Badger's probable reign of terror would last, but I sensed an arduous battle with casualties; I was just trying to avoid being toted out of my office in a body bag.

As I pondered this latest development I couldn't help but see the irony in all this bullshit. Here was yet another "leasing asshole" trying to make my life miserable; I resolved to be on top of my game and stay alert; a "backstabbing advisory" was in effect and I didn't foresee smooth sailing any time soon.

Before Ernie paid me that visit, as I previously mentioned, he had just completed a whirlwind tour of most of the core cities of the Group, making painstaking and somewhat meaningless visits to even some of our most remote locations. His three-day whirlwind tour in the field was split between our two newly promoted Group Rental Managers (new titles and increased responsibilities), Dick Jansen and Scott Kendrick.

Ernie really liked Dick and was quite impressed with his knowledge and enthusiasm, and that was great; within two months Dick would be promoted to run the Austin based portion of Texas, while his old buddy, Tony Moist would be shipped off to run San Antonio; this coming in the wake of the Larry Herrera firing, a guy who originally worked under Andy Jansky in Houston, before being promoted to run San Antonio and its surrounding areas.

It was starting to become commonplace to see Groups that were fairly spread out, geographically, with large fleet sizes to be chopped up, and that's precisely what happened with that particular Texas Group.

With Ernie's vote of confidence, Dick was a lock to get promoted. On the other hand, Ernie was not impressed with Scott. According to our micro-managing corporate drone, Scott didn't show Ernie a very good level of enthusiasm and seemed bored and disinterested in anything Ernie had to say. Badger had praised Dick for taking copious notes the entire time Ernie was with him (cleverly sucking up), while Scott never wrote a fucking thing down (not so clever).

Obviously, Scott misjudged Ernie, and took him lightly. I never asked Dick what he did with all those notes he took, but I'm sure he put them to good use.

Ernie continued his criticism by saying Scott had a "surfer-boy haircut" and didn't like the fact that Scott was always sneaking out of the office on Wednesdays to play golf with his cronies. Poor Scott was blamed for what Dick was doing. Ernie got the wrong information; Scott was a slightly better golfer than Dick, but Dick played with much more regularity, usually for free, and usually on Wednesdays.

But, unfortunately for Scott, when talking to him, his combination Texas and Louisiana drawl, belied his demeanor, which indeed reflected sort of a California cool "surfer boy" mentality; it was fast times at Enterprise high and Scott was Spicoli, just looking for a good buzz and some tasty waves, man.

Scott was the only person that I'd ever come across in the history of Enterprise who always, and I mean always referred to females as "chicks". It didn't matter what age or ethnicity, Scott was an equal opportunity "surfer boy"; all females were "chicks" and that was all there was to it.

I could never quite get Scott to understand, there were many females, such as grandmothers, First Ladies, the Queen of England, six month old babies, employees, or customers who really shouldn't be called "chicks". His lingo persisted, unabated; and at this particular period of rough sailing for the West Group, it didn't help his cause with Ernie, who more than likely heard "chick" coming out of Scott's surfer boy mouth a time or two, and who was looking to pick apart any aspect of the operation that didn't seem appropriate.

Ernie was relentless. Not long after this micro-managing and tedious visit, Ernie came up with the bright idea of "regionalizing" the Group; which essentially entailed increasing overhead, and reducing profits, all in the name of "opportunity".

The process he was talking about would come about in due time; however, at this particular time it was about as appropriate as calling every female in the world a "chick". When I balked at this suggestion, Ernie couldn't believe it. I held my autonomous ground, but it was getting shakier by the moment.

Clearly, Ernie Badger would never be in my camp; I felt like a prisoner in corporate hell, and I'd stay in jail as long as Ernie was the warden.

Less than a month after we experienced Ernie's stressful visit, serious trouble started brewing in Northern Arizona. About five years earlier, we opened our first location in Flagstaff, inside a dealership by the name of McCoy Motors. Dick had a chick (whose name totally escapes me and, sorry, I couldn't resist) working for him in Tucson who expressed an interest in moving up there, so off she went. To help her out, since initially, she would've been completely on her own, we agreed to bring her husband on board (whose name totally escapes me), primarily as a car prep, and jack-of-all-trades.

Things seemed to be going fairly well, and the business gradually grew. Before we knew it, the husband started taking on more responsibility, was now taking care of customers, as well as learning some of the other stuff you need to know to justify making him a full-time management trainee.

Over the years, this dude and chick duo would open a few more branches, hire some marginal to average employees, and meander along, without really making that deal work very well.

Dick and I decided we needed some stronger leadership up there, so a go-getter from Tucson, Jerry McNabb, accepted the challenge to become Northern Arizona's first City Manager. The husband and wife team, after an arduous and heated debate with Dick and I, refused to agree with our position (as is their right), and attempted to get their handful of employees to join the little mutiny they were planning. That didn't work because these poor frazzled employees were getting tired of their unjustified whining, and wanted Jerry to come on board. It got to be quite a mess.

In the end, we were forced to end their little mutiny by making them "walk the plank". Naturally, the second they get fired, they do the whole wrongful termination thing, we settle out of court, and everybody lived happily ever after.

To Ernie's credit, he supported our decision to get rid of these two although he had to throw in a little jab about what a bad decision it was to allow the husband to work there to begin with. Maybe he was right, but at the time, when we were trying to launch that operation, we needed all the help we could get.

Meanwhile, as the Flagstaff Fiasco is under way, Dick gets the promotion to Austin, and I'm then immersed in the long process of interviewing candidates to fill the vacancy in Tucson. After I hired Dave Hummel, a fine young man who was working in Ohio at the time, and got him into place in Tucson, my corporate oppressor retreats to his bunker to regroup; I suppose it was time for him to focus his fury on other Groups.

I had survived the initial assault. However, I never felt comfortable, since I never knew if a sneak attack was imminent; it didn't materialize as 1995 ended and 1996 began, but there would be trouble on the horizon.

The 1995 Fall Officers Meeting, the big one that includes chicks/spouses, was held in St Louis, primarily so we could take a tour of the new corporate administrative facility that had been recently completed, located on the outskirts of Clayton on land that used to house the St Louis County Hospital. There was no doubt this marked a new era for Enterprise, as the company had already overtaken Hertz for the top spot in terms of rental cars in service, and now needed to expand the headquarters to keep up with the incredible growth; the era of big corporate bureaucracy had officially arrived, and the epicenter was now at 600 Corporate Park Drive, in Clayton, Missouri, 63105.

Andy Taylor got a lot of national attention with interviews on those various business programs on cable, primarily discussing the business strategies that got Enterprise to that number one position. Watching him confidently answering questions with genuine Mid-western humility made me feel proud to be working for such a great company. Andy was cool and of course, had a nice tan, to boot.

The meetings themselves were slightly awkward, as quite a few of the Enterprise couples were offering their condolences about my marital problems, with the pained expressions on their faces that reflected the anguish they thought I felt. What these well-intentioned people didn't understand was I was actually happy now, and I wasn't worried about things like showing up for this thing with no, uh chick.

Kicking off the proceedings every year is a nice dinner, preceded by cocktails. This gives everybody the chance to mingle with their pals who they may only see a couple of times a year. Looking around that very crowded room, I generally dashed in and out of the small groups of cronies, said a few witty things, and then quickly slid away. This usually kept me from being trapped by anyone wanting to offer condolences, and I could spot that look anywhere from thirty to forty paces, depending on how sad they looked.

The clones had their lovely, and in some cases, sullen wives dressed up in their elegant attire, and I noticed quite a few couples seemed not so particularly happy, based on little things I knew about body language. But there they were, together at this very important Enterprise meeting, which was really more of a social gathering than business function on that first evening. However, in the minds of many nervous Officers, attending this particular meeting without a spouse could be hazardous to their career health.

A very nice man who at least for the time being, was the corporate human resources manager, Jerry Sparks, approached me with the look of bereavement in his eyes; his sneak attack caught me by surprise; he made eye contact with me while I became distracted by his famous hair-do, a classic comb-over look that was popular with the "in denial" balding segment of society, but was falling out of favor for the simple but elegant Charles Barkley look. Soon, even guys with full heads of hair shaved it anyway, to look cooler.

I was trapped; I knew I was going to be subjected to another round of well-intentioned, but unnecessary sympathy. As he sadly looked at me, he began, "Larry, you've got to feel awful being here with no wife. I just heard that Pam's not here. I'm so sorry you have to go through all of this."

I liked Jerry; he was genuine, although at this particular moment, awkward, especially with that folic challenged hair, which was so meticulously wrapped, around that mostly bald, head that I was now closely examining while Jerry continued his sympathetic monologue.

For his sake, I bravely accepted his sincere condolences, "Jerry; thanks for your encouragement. Yeah, it's tough, but with the support from my friends, I'll get through it." I couldn't think of anything else to say.

He then slowly placed his right hand on my left shoulder, another awkward move at best, while I tried to fix my sincere gaze right into his sad human resources eyes; neither of us blinking at all; then, in a moment of weakness; I snuck another peek up at that plastered hair wrapped around his noggin and that signaled the end to our chat.

"Well, Jerry; I guess I'd better go eat my dinner. I'll see you around; and thanks again."

I gave him the best and bravest smile a poor guy like me could muster under these trying circumstances. Jerry felt better knowing that he cheered me up. As he turned, rubbed his eyes, and slowly walked away with that that resourceful long-legged human resources stride, I thought this helps explain why the divorce rate among Officers in the company is so low, and wondered if he would ever realize how bad his hair looked, and take the only action he could possibly take to improve his look.

"Just shave it, Jerry", I thought to myself, as I made a mad dash for the buffet. "Just shave it."

Chapter 22
The Standard Rent-A-Car Acquisition Fiasco

W hen Doug Brown switched Salt Lake City and Sacramento for Fresno and Bakersfield, to complete the configuration of the West Group that seemed like a bad trade to me. I didn't even get a player to be named later. Instead I got the fiercest competitor we've ever had in a local market in Standard Rent-a-Car.

What Standard had going for them was a passion for marketing their service, providing very good customer service, and getting very involved in community service. This was a winning formula since Burl and Etta Houck founded the Fresno based company back in 1970. Burl supplied the capital, played golf, and smiled a lot; Etta got in everybody's face and said they had to use Standard or she'd be very upset.

Burl and Etta had three sons who ran different divisions of the business, Ed, Tom, and Dave. Dave was the head-honcho in charge of the rental operations, and he was the guy who just happened to be calling me at their office when I was returning a rental car during my first visit to Fresno in 1987. I thought I had snuck into town undetected, but their undercover work was exceptional.

"Mr. Underwood, I've got Dave Houck on the line, and he'd like to speak with you."

After a pleasant little chat in which he tried to find out what I was up to, I told him about 175; seriously, I never told him a thing, of course; because divulging trade secrets was something Officers never did. Hell, I didn't even have any secrets to divulge anyway.

The purpose of that phone call was to try to intimidate me, of all people; to make me think that there was no way we'd ever beat them, unless of course, we gave them a lot of money, but that would be the only way.

Well, I'm here to tell you, that beat them we did; in a very humane way with lots of money; lots and lots of money. When the soon to be departed Brian Meade and I came to town with an office all lined up, and cars, and everything else necessary to start renting those cars, we thought we'd pay Dave Houck a little surprise visit, to see how he liked it.

He showed no emotion at all, and almost laughed when we initiated a conversation that went something like, "Dave, do you want us to buy you out now, or later?" After careful consideration (lasting about one second) he said, "Later", and that's what came to pass, nearly a decade later.

However, it's possible that little visit from the two of us helped a little bit, from a psychological standpoint, although not likely.

The Houck family did know one thing for sure; Enterprise simply wasn't going to go away ever. We were ageless; Burl and Etta were old and getting even older, so they were very serious about bailing out of the business, if the price was right.

The price Enterprise ultimately paid was so "right" Burl and Etta never stopped laughing all the way to the bank, to their country club, or anywhere else went, for that matter.

In the long run, the inflated price Enterprise paid to get Standard out of the business was justified; but for the first year or two it sucked, big time.

When news of the buyout was sprung on me, I happened to be in St Louis, visiting family. After a few phone calls, Ernie Badger tracks me down at my dad's house. When I heard his voice on the other end, I was thinking, "I'm on vacation and I don't want to talk to him." However, I knew something pretty significant was forthcoming, but I sure as hell didn't expect the news he laid on me.

"Larry, I've got some good news. We've bought out Standard Rent-a-Car." He then went into some sort of monologue about the perseverance, hard work, and dedication our people had to make this all possible. I agreed.

There was much to talk about so I drove to the corporate office all dressed up in my blue jeans to talk to Ernie, and the architect of this huge takeover, Bill Hole. Bill was now a corporate big shot and we had long since buried the hatchet over the Brian Meade debacle; well, at least I had.

It was a somewhat unusual environment in the corporate offices when some of the drones or other corporate worker bees spotted me dressed up like I was going to a ball game; and when they saw me slide into Bill Hole's office, along with Ernie Badger, there's no telling what the corporate rumor mill was grinding out at that moment. However, I appeared to be way too chipper to be getting the ax, especially after leaving the sanctuary whistling a happy tune; I'm sure nothing about that scene made much sense to anybody else in that tense office, aside from Andy Taylor or Don Ross, whom I didn't even recall seeing; I was so preoccupied about this major acquisition.

As Bill and Ernie rolled me through this thing, I kept asking what the price tag was going to be for the West Group. Bill, the architect of the buyout did most of the talking; I'd get complicated, multi-tiered responses that seemed to skirt the issue; there were so many variables, he'd say, and it depends on whether we buy any of their cars and what the used car market would be, and everything. I was still in the dark, but I realized whatever the cost it was a done deal and that would be that.

With Fresno about ready to double the size of its fleet, I rehashed the conversation Ernie and I had about a year earlier, when he was badgering me to prematurely "regionalize" the Group, and I thought certainly to do that at this particular moment seemed obvious. Ernie abruptly said, "Don't worry about that now. We need to make the official announcement to the company before we even think about that."

That was the catch. This was mid July, and these guys insisted on keeping this secret from everybody for another month or so. I couldn't tell Scott Kendrick, Brett Todd, or anybody else for that matter, unless I wanted the death penalty.

To me, it seemed illogical to keep this a secret from the two guys who would be most involved in all aspects of this takeover from our end. It also seemed illogical to have this whole thing unfold in the late summer when it was imprudent, from a fleet management perspective, to be adding cars to our fleet right before the new models were about to hit the streets. The cars that would be added would depreciate at a very accelerated rate when the new models hit, and for us that's not good news for our bottom lines when we have to eventually sell those fucking sleds.

Secrecy ruled the upper echelon of Enterprise; sometimes it seemed very appropriate and sometimes not so appropriate. When Hole was busily negotiating this deal with the Houck family, I think he should've gotten the three General Managers who would be affected by this deal involved, at least quietly. With our input, maybe he wouldn't have spent so much of our money just to get them out of the business. Maybe he should've waited a couple of months to let the used car market fall, before pulling the trigger; instead, the cars we were forced to buy from Standard were high mileage sleds that were purchased at the peak of the used car market; so Standard made out like bandits, and we were mugged.

It would take us nearly two years to recover from the financial setback in Fresno, and we had to do a lot of shucking and jiving to keep our commissioned employees from quitting in a state of total disillusionment.

We now had twice as many cars in our Fresno/Bakersfield fleet, twice as many problems, and half as much profit. But we would eventually become a regionalized Group, and after getting our expenses in line, became one of the top performing Groups in the entire company.

However, in the late summer of 1996, we were still in a state of flux. The big "roll out" which was going to be announced by corporate as soon as they got the official okay from the Houck family to announce the take-over, would turn out to be a fucking nightmare.

Late one summer afternoon, I was visiting the Las Vegas airport branch, and at that time, nobody knew about this deal yet. Suddenly, Scott Bridger, the branch manager comes over shakes my hand, and says, "Congratulations, I just read the message sent out by Hole that you guys bought out Standard. Way to go!"

This secret deal was no longer a secret, and it was only 4 pm in the west, meaning it was 6 pm in St Louis. The only problem was, corporate was supposed to wait until after 8pm in St Louis, to allow the Standard employees time to find out from the Houck family that the Evil Empire had taken over. This was already getting sloppy; it looked to me like nobody in St Louis wanted to stay in the office that late.

Somebody at corporate must've immediately caught the mistake. With the inter-company message system, any "sent" message could be deleted as long as it was never opened by the recipient. Bam; in less than one minute, the message disappeared from workstations all over the world, and hardly a soul even noticed.

Finally, the official announcement was sent out again; by someone on overtime, and then, the not so fabulous roll out plan was announced. It involved the take-over of the Standard offices bright and early the next morning by the smiling Enterprise enemy, carrying boxes of donuts as a show of good will to what we hoped would be future Enterprise employees among the old Standard gang.

Credibility became a major issue with their old employees; for years, it had been pounded into their heads (primarily from Etta Houck) that Enterprise was the Evil Empire, so the reaction from these poor ex-SRAC employees was understandably a blend of shock, grief, disillusionment, and horror.

So yes, a funny thing happened on the way to the take-over. Nobody from Standard's corporate hierarchy (they had a small one) really bothered to tell the vast majority of their old employees that the good guys would be invading their offices at 8am. The Houck family told their upper echelon managers, but apparently decided to blow off the rest of the employees, because after all, it really wasn't their problem.

As our apprehensive employees are trying to reassure the now former Standard employees who are looking like hogs on the verge of slaughter, that it was all good total bedlam ensued. Sobbing and/or pissed off former Standard workers, in droves, were calling Dave Houck for an explanation. Dave, in turn, calls Hole to tell him the roll out plan wasn't rolling out as planned; but perhaps the Houck family should have better informed the troops prior to this moment.

While all this insanity was taking place in Fresno, I was on a surrealistic conference call with Ernie, Bill, and the two other California General Managers being affected by this deal, Susie Ire (Sacramento) and Bob Caspar (San Francisco). Initially, the tone is upbeat and everything seems to be going as planned for the first thirty seconds or so of the roll out.

Suddenly, Ernie sternly tells me, "Larry, Bill and I need to talk to you on another line." Obviously, something was wrong, and I was pretty sure it was going to be my fault. They decided the reason all this shit was happening was because I wasn't in Fresno. I was first admonished for not being there; after all, what good is a riot without me being there? Then I was instructed to get on the next flight over there to restore some order. After all, if anybody can stop this madness, it would be me.

Actually, I wasn't in Fresno on the day of the inquisition I mean acquisition not just because I was asked by Dave Houck to hold off for a day or two to let the dust settle. He knew things would be tumultuous, but what actually happened was far beyond any run of the mill tumultuousness I'd ever seen. As far as the family was concerned, dealing with us was not all that important, as they knew they had the money coming, regardless.

The primary reason I wasn't in Fresno on the big day of the revolt was because the evening before I had a pre-arranged dinner meeting in Las Vegas with some corporate car sales manager, along with my Group Car Sale Manager. If I blew these guys off, I was envisioning old Ernie questioning my commitment to this very important department; so I don't think there was any way to win that one.

Over the next few days, we got things stabilized in Fresno; I gave an upbeat, inspiring, and appropriately humorous speech to the old Standard employees (I even had my very own microphone and podium, just like the good old days), trying to recruit them for Enterprise, and most of them actually made the switch.

Out of necessity, we bought hundreds of their high mileage pieces of shit to add to our fleet at the peak of the used car market. Within a couple of months, we were more upside down on these sleds than somebody who bought nothing but NASDAQ stocks in early 2000, and sold them right after 9/11.

Although stability had been restored in Fresno, from a morale standpoint, the financial terms of the buyout would clearly be a challenge for us to overcome for quite some time; I now had my first experience of the inevitable backstabbing syndrome that so often happens when things like this don't go quite as well as the corporate architect of this plan had hoped.

By mid October, I would be fighting for my Enterprise life, as my corporate tormentor, Ernie Badger, was now armed and dangerous, and intending to inflict serious and potentially fatal back wounds on Uncle Larry.

Luckily for me, as it turned out, this guy was a pretty incompetent backstabber.

Chapter 23
Backstabbing, Part I

After the Standard Rent-a-Car debacle, I was preparing to wage a survival battle with Ernie, and more than likely, his corporate boss, Bill Hole. I was guardedly optimistic as I headed to the "spouses included" Fall Officers Meeting in Florida. After all, we'd won our war with Standard, although for now, it was a pyrrhic victory; but nevertheless it was heroic and I knew I'd get a few pats on the back from the fellow Officers, including the big guys, Jack, Andy, and Don.

Before heading to the meeting, I had the experience of receiving my "annual review" from that master of business, Ernie Badger. I'd been a General Manager for over ten years by then, and I'd had two other "annual reviews", one performed by Doug Brown in '87, one by Mark Miller in '92, and now this one. Without sounding pessimistic, I'd already surmised the reason for the review at this particular time was to have some documentation in my personnel file that I sucked, and with any luck, be gone before the company had to spend any money for me to attend the meeting.

That was the harsh reality I was facing. I knew Ernie didn't like anything about me, but I had no idea he was so bad at writing reviews or really anything, for that matter, and I believe it was this unusual lack of writing skills for such a high level employee, that kind of bailed me out of a tough situation.

I really had no idea he was illiterate. When he spoke, he used proper grammar and sounded like he knew what he was talking about.

When Ernie wrote, however, he forgot to end his sentences, or at least put the proper punctuation in them. His syntax was downright sinful, and his thought process was mysterious; it was almost impossible to tell if he was happy with something or unhappy.

Ernie's total lack of comprehending the separation between personal and business life was more than likely the coupe de grace to his downfall and my escape route. When I read what he wrote on my review, I almost laughed out loud; I also realized it was pretty much illegal, although I never said a word about that, nor in my written response did I go ballistic. I didn't think that was necessary.

Aside from criticizing everything I did from a business standpoint, in a rambling incoherent sort of way, he thought he'd step in and tell me that my "personal life was not heading in the right direction". As I clutched this written diatribe, I asked him to kindly elaborate on what he meant about my "personal life". I knew whatever he would say, I'd relish. I'd already begun mentally preparing my written comments to his disjointed and haphazard attacks, and felt pretty good about my chances of successfully refuting his bullshit. I reflected back to the disapproving look on his face about a year and a half ago when I told him I was separated. I could hardly wait for him to start babbling now.

Ernie gave me a condescending look that reminded me of how the lease salesmen would look at the guys in daily reptile cleaning those reptiles many years ago. His blunt words snapped me out of that moment; "Larry, come on. Everybody knows you've got a stable of women!" The absurdity of that comment was so lusciously stupid, but alas, untrue; I just looked at him in amazement, leaned forward and just blurted one word, "What!"

Yes, I wish I did have a stable of women, but I never could line that deal up. I felt good that Ernie was somehow jealous of me, so I really didn't put up much of an argument, because this line of crap that he thought was going to cause me trouble, I felt now would work in my favor. However, even though I knew for sure that he was a complete idiot, he was still dangerous. After all, he was still a corporate something or other, and technically, he was my boss; and without a doubt, he was going to do everything in his awkward power to backstab me out of the company; although by this time his knives were dull butter knives.

I submitted my written reply (which would be promptly read by Don Ross) by the next day, and I think it was pretty well worded. It was subtle, understated, and carved through Ernie's pathetic mess like a person with a very sharp knife, not a dull butter knife, cutting through a pathetic mess, or something. Uh.

I think Ernie had all but been disarmed; essentially by what he had written on that sheet of paper; combined with my well thought out response to his bullshit.

As it would turn out, I would have one more backstabbing attempt to thwart immediately after the Fall Officers Meeting, and I'd be home free, sooner than I imagined possible.

Chapter 24

Misery Had Company

After making the long trip to Miami, taking the shuttle to the hotel, checking in, shuffling over to my hotel room, and unpacking my little carry on bag, I realized I was so preoccupied with my future with Enterprise that I'd forgotten to pack any golf shorts, which would be a necessity for this particular Fall Officers Meeting. Whenever free from the dreaded business break out sessions, golf would be on the agenda. Now that's my kind of meeting.

I was just hoping I wouldn't have to endure another round with my pal, Ernie the "stable master"; and it had nothing to do with his perplexing approach to writing; it was his annoying approach to golf that had me agitated, as thoughts of his slow, deliberate, and inexcusably ineffective play at Pebble Beach a few years earlier, raced through my head. For crying out loud, if you're a horrible golfer, at least have the decency to play quickly.

Fortunately, I was never placed in his foursome during the entire meeting; in fact, I don't even remember seeing him at all, until the last day when I was on the practice green and he came over babbling about something. I stayed focused on my putting stroke, never looking at him, and when forced to respond to his babble, would use one-word answers, hoping that would end the interview, and it seemed to work. He stopped talking, and then suddenly, he was gone.

With plenty of time to kill before the opening reception and dinner, I thought I'd pop into one of the hotel bars and find somebody to vent with. Coincidentally, the first person I saw was Dennis Reinhardt, Atlanta's General Manager, who was another one of my assistant managers back in my St Louis days. I always liked Dennis and I told him I thought he was as good as anybody I saw in rental, aside from Andy Jansky, but he made the switch to leasing, saying it was more challenging.

I don't remember why, but he always called me "Lars". I always called him "Bones", a mocking tribute to some lame assistant I had before Dennis, who called him "Bonehead", then later shortened it to "Bones". The guy thought he was being clever; we just thought he was a dumb ass; I think his name was Bill, and as I recall, he was the only person in the rental department that ever caused me to lose my temper to the point of hollering at him. I hollered at a few of the leasing people, but not too many, and only if they hollered at me first.

After getting through our normal greeting ritual, the topic quickly turned to Ernie Badger, who also happened to be Reinhardt's CVP. When I told Dennis about some of the trouble I'd had with Ernie, he told me, "Larry, the guy is killing me." I was a little bit surprised because I always thought they were pretty good friends. Dennis really looked down in the dumps; and I suppose I was too; so we told each other to hang in there, that we'd probably get somebody else one of these days, and it would have to be an improvement; but Dennis added, "I don't know how much longer I can last with this guy." I had that same feeling.

Despite carving him up with my rebuttal on the lamest review I'd ever seen, I still never felt comfortable with him lurking around. I gave a quick look around the hotel bar, expecting to see him lurking around somewhere.

156

Later on, I briefly ran into Houston's General Manager, John Ebeling. John was a colorful character who had been around forever. He was one of the original General Managers to be promoted to President, but he hardly acted like an ostentatious leasing asshole. I liked him but I knew he held a slight grudge against me for whisking Pam away from his Group over a decade ago; still, he was always cordial, and at times, quite funny.

At this particular time, the festivities were about to begin, the Officers and their wives were swarming all over, so the time for real conversation was over; John and I just gave each other good-natured smiles and nods, while shaking hands; we both quickly moved on to greet other cohorts.

Inside of a week, unbeknownst to me, I'd rid myself of Ernie's anal retentive, micro-managing, borderline illiterate ass; and the first person to call me to find out what magic I was able to work, was none other than John Ebeling, who was still saddled with his nemesis. I'll never forget his words; "Larry, how did you do it? He's driving us bat shits!"

Chapter 25
Prelude To The Inevitable Showdown

f it weren't for the fact that I was preoccupied about the prospects of getting shooed out the door by my corporate pest control specialist, and therefore quite possibly been attending my last Fall Officers Meeting, I probably would have enjoyed it more.

However, thanks to Jack Taylor's personal contribution to this particular meeting, the 1996 version of the Fall Dog and Pony Show probably had more positive impact on the company than all the other meetings combined.

In recent years, as Jack got a little older, he was content to stay in the background, while listening to what was being discussed; and generally speaking he agreed with the resolutions to any pertinent issues.

He certainly felt uncomfortable with the adoration that nearly everyone had for him, and from time to time felt obligated to give a little speech which usually lasted less than five or ten seconds. This was a truly humble man who genuinely appreciated what his employees created for him. On the rare occasions he spoke, he'd always seem to wrap it up with "I love you all; thank you."

Everybody loved Jack, and aside from mom and dad, everybody respected him more than just about anybody they knew in the whole wide world.

On the first night of the festivities, which were held outside in perfect weather under that moon over Miami, it seemed like everybody was feeling very jovial, and maybe even a little smug; the company had just posted excellent profit numbers, business was still booming, there would be a lot of golf to be played in paradise, and optimism reigned supreme.

The raucous Enterprise laughter that signifies all is well, reverberated throughout that balmy south Florida resort known as Turnbury Isle. Cigars were being lit left and right, and smoke billowed up towards the heavens while the joyful sounds continued.

After Andy Taylor pleasantly welcomed us to another Fall Officers Meeting, introduced the handful of new Officers attending for the very first time, and said a few more nice business-sounding platitudes, he turned the podium over to his father.

As Jack Taylor made the short three-stride walk to the podium, to the usual standing ovation, the smug Officers and their equally smug spouses gazed at him in admiration, wondering what sort of pleasant comments he'd be making this evening.

Nobody was prepared for what would happen next.

The smiles of those smug Officers and spouses slowly dissipated, as the tone in Jack's voice was stern and foreboding. Suddenly, the only audible sounds were the clattering of dishes and eating utensils being whisked away by the hotel staff, who were totally oblivious to anything being said by some rich dude to a bunch of rich white dudes and their chicks.

Clearly, something was bothering Jack that he wanted known to every Officer in the company; and most of all, he wanted it fixed.

A couple of years earlier, the Enterprise brain trust devised a system to measure customer satisfaction, called the "Enterprise Service Quality index" (ESQi). When the numbers were computed and distributed to the Enterprise Groups each month, whoever was towards the bottom of the heap felt the wrath of corporate, unless of course, they were at or near the top of the heap, from a profit standpoint.

Frequently, Southern California would be near the bottom of the ESQi list, but nobody seemed to mind; they were making so much profit it really didn't seem to matter. Groups with high ESQi scores seemed to be heavily weighted in the South or in remote areas, causing some cynics to jokingly comment, "Those hillbillies are happy if there's no pig shit in the driver's seat." Back and forth the comments flew, justifying ESQi scores to suit whatever position they wanted to advocate. Not many people took it too seriously. I overhead a few of my colleagues sneering about their bad scores, while their cohorts chortled and guffawed along with them, "Well, they don't pay me on ESQi; they pay me to fucking make money!"

That philosophy changed overnight.

Jack knew many of the Officers present thought ESQi to be a joke, and the recent scores reflected that sentiment. The company's passion for customer service was falling by the wayside, ironically, as profits soared. Sooner or later, however, the bubble was going to burst, and Jack knew it.

Philosophically, Jack's number one "core value" for his company is, quite simply, providing absolutely the best service to his customers as humanly possible; and it now rankled him to see so many top ranking employees; and most of them were right there, by now, with their mouths agape; brushing this aside with the disdain of shooing a house fly away.

Jack sternly addressed the gathering, and in no uncertain terms said, "We have to immediately improve our customer service ratings in each and every Group in the company, and if we don't, we'll bring in replacements who will improve it." That brief statement was very clear to everyone, as many mouths remained open, yet mute.

No one doubted his passion; no one wanted to get fired, and the company's customer service quality index steadily rose each year throughout the end of my career. Getting a promotion no longer solely depended on how well that person helped generate strong profits; without the accompanying good ESQi scores, they'd have to try again some other time.

On the last night of festivities, I made a point to have a quick visit with Andy Taylor to show him how nice and tan I was, and how well dressed I was (actually I was). He once again apologized for putting me through the anguish of sticking his cousin on me, while admiring my sharp executive image; which of course, is some more total bullshit.

Actually, he simply gave me the obligatory "congratulations" for helping dethrone the former King of the San Joaquin Valley, and I quickly responded that we were now ready to regionalize the Group. Naturally, I was looking for some words of encouragement from Jack's son, Andy; and he delivered them; very simply saying, "Great; go for it!"

By the time I got back to the office the following Monday, I was ready to "go for it", but one of the first inter-company messages I received was from the relentless Ernie Badger. It read something to the effect that there were so many administrative problems in the Group they would probably be sending an audit team to get to the bottom of the mess; give me a fucking break.

I suppose that meant I couldn't "go for it" now.

Becoming more that a little agitated by now, I immediately replied, "Ernie, you say we have administrative problems and we're trying to address them by getting the regionalization process going. I spoke to Andy Taylor (clever name dropping I thought) at the meeting, and he told me to go for it. I'm a little confused. When can we expect to get corporate approval to finally regionalize the Group, which of course, would greatly reduce the administrative problems?"

I almost felt like I was conversing with a six year-old child, who was made an honorary Corporate Vice President for the day as part of a special field trip to a big company.

Not long after I sent that note, I receive Ernie's reply, which I'm guessing wasn't meant for me, especially since my name is not "Bill". It read, "Bill, we may have a problem here. Larry thinks because Andy said okay, that meant he's okay. Let's get together and discuss our strategy on how we're going to handle Larry."

Unfortunately for Ernie, in his haste to backstab me, he inadvertently forwarded the message right back to me, instead of Bill. Even though the stupidity of my corporate clown had now approached epic proportions, he was still dangerous; however, I couldn't resist letting him know that I knew what he was plotting; or at least, trying to plot.

I immediately wrote back, "Ernie, this is a real Catch 22. You say we have administrative problems, and I say the best way to address that is to regionalize, yet you won't let us."

I should have then added, "Oh, by the way, where did you learn how to write? You come across like some stupid third grader."

About twenty minutes later, a flustered Ernie calls me up, and after a very heated discussion, tells me to fly to St Louis, so he can meet with me the following morning. The conversation continues, and by this time, I don't give a shit about anything; I pretty much thought this was going to be the end of the line, so whatever crap he dished my way, I gave it back to him in spades, very loudly.

When I go to baseball games, I'm the guy you can hear anywhere in the ballpark. My voice just seems to carry, and I'm sure on this particular day in my office, talking to Ernie Badger, my entire administrative staff, upstairs and downstairs, where I was positioned, heard me loud and clear.

When the conversation finally ended, I was a bit hoarse, but still very feisty. I slammed the phone down quite hard, causing my cheesy little plastic Enterprise phone rest to pop off about five feet straight up in the air, coming to rest almost back in its original position; the moment was a brief humorous respite for me (I'm easily amused) and inspired me to give the office with a little dose of my sarcastic false bravado, "This might be it for Uncle Larry!"

In reality, that's exactly what I thought. I immediately walked next door into a stunned Dave Vogt's office, and just said, "We'll see what happens."

Chapter 26

A Compromising Reprieve

I hopped on the first available flight to St Louis, shortly after my telephone confrontation with the most awkward backstabber in Enterprise history, although there are no official records posted on that.

Mentally, I had my bases covered; it was just a matter of whether or not logic would prevail over illogic.

I arrived several minutes early the next morning for my scheduled badgering, and was directed to a meeting room where Ernie was already comfortably positioned, and looking very dapper, as usual. I was encouraged by the fact that he was the only one there, but I still had no idea what was in store for me.

Ernie immediately began by telling me he would no longer be my Corporate Vice President, and that Tim Welsh would take over in that capacity. I looked at him, never saying a word, and nodded my acknowledgement.

Then, as he began assaulting the business management side of the Group, I realized where this was leading. Dave Vogt had to go, unconditionally. This came as no surprise, as the frequency of complaints about Dave from John O'Connell (the head of corporate accounting) and his underlings had escalated dramatically over the past year.

It seemed to me this was a decision reached by the corporate hierarchy as a compromising solution to the mess Ernie had created. In exchange for not bringing me down, Vogt was now the sacrificial lamb, which gave Ernie the chance to save face with the corporation, as well as the Groups in the field who might've been wondering what was going on; with Vogt's sudden departure, having Ernie move on to another Group seemed plausible; after all, his mission in the West had been accomplished.

With Ernie's enormous ego badly bruised, he wanted to launch a few more verbal assaults in my direction, and I was glad to give him whatever satisfaction he derived from this bullshit. By this point, I barely heard a word he was saying, and made little attempt to pretend like anything he said really mattered, because it didn't.

In less than one hour, the session was over. As I was preparing to walk out of that meeting room, I looked Ernie right in the eye and said, "Believe it or not, Ernie; dealing with you has made me a stronger person; and I believe, a better manager. For that, I thank you."

On the trip back to Phoenix, I felt relieved to have survived with a fresh start, although I knew my slate would never be clean. It would only be a matter of time before another assault would be launched in my direction; after all, that's life under the corporate microscope.

Now I faced the responsibility of telling the guy who had the guts to hook on with the pathetic little start-up West Group, ten years ago, that it was time for him to go.

The day after Clinton's resounding victory over Bob Dole, I walked into the humble West Group administrative office, and made that first abrupt right turn that led to Dave Vogt's working quarters. As I closed the door, Dave who was still seated at his desk, busily at work, with papers scattered everywhere, looked up and simply asked, "How'd it go?"

"Dave, I've got to let you go. O'Connell and his people will never be a supporter of you going forward, and that's all there is to it. My bullshit with Ernie is over and I've got my job and a new CVP; but for you, all I can say is, I'll get you the best severance package for a Controller in the history of Enterprise."

With tears in his eyes, he shook his head in disbelief, looked down for a moment, then looked back up at me and said, "Okay; thanks."

Chapter 27
Building Greater Success

On the date Bill Clinton clobbered Bob Dole to earn another four year term as our cigar smoking philandering President, I emerged victorious from the Ernie Badger mud-slinging campaign, happy to still be gainfully employed, and optimistic about the future, which coincidentally, would amount to another four year term as the leader of the West Group.

Of course in most business situations, the duration of a career is an unknown quantity; it could end tomorrow or go on for even more than four years; but after this great escape that was the least of my concerns; I just wanted to get down to business again.

Freed from the shackles of malicious micro-managing (at least temporarily), I was eagerly preparing for the next step; getting a strong, newly structured, management team in place, while relocating the administrative office to Las Vegas, Nevada; entertainment capital of Enterprise Rent-a-Car, and I suppose, the rest of the world.

Tim Welsh, a guy I really didn't know much about was my new Corporate Vice President; Mike Andera, a talented Controller from Seattle, via Southern California, took over the business management responsibilities, and the four Regional Vice Presidents were yet to be determined, although I already had a good idea who I wanted to snag.

From outside the Group, there were two very strong candidates who clearly had the best credentials, Mark Tobiassen and Darren Gottschalk.

I'd known Mark for a number of years from the rental managers meetings, and at six feet nine inches in height, he was hard to miss. He was a very intelligent and thoughtful, nice guy with a good sense of humor.

He looked like a college philosophy professor who would lead his intramural basketball team to victory against teams like "Dorm C-2", usually by a score in the neighborhood of 124 to 14, and he would account for 50 or 60 effortless points himself. I used to be the star of Dorm C-2, averaging almost four points and one rebound per game.

Darren was a pretty good-sized fellow himself, good looking, well spoken, and one of the best all-round athletes I ever saw at Enterprise. He was a big, strong guy who once had a very brief shot at professional football, playing as a replacement tight end for the Raiders during the strike marred '87 NFL campaign; he had a very gregarious personality, and never seemed to be short on hilarious stories; I forgot to ask him if he ever met Shane Falco; but wait, that replacement was a fictitious quarterback; but I still loved the movie ("The Replacements").

Who could ever forget Keanu Reaves' classic line at the end of the movie, as he's in the huddle preparing for that last game winning play, "Gentlemen; it has been an honor sharing the field of battle with you." But Gene Hackman probably had the best line in the movie when he said, simply, "Winners always want the ball when the game's on the line."

I really liked both Gottschalk and Tobiassen, as they were not only knowledgeable about the business, and they were quite eager to work for a General Manager known for giving autonomy to his managers; and they both wanted the ball.

I was quite fortunate they were still around, after Detroit had only recently regionalized themselves, and the talent pool had diminished, but Mark never considered going there to begin with, and Darren was for some reason, not chosen for one of the four openings.

I then promoted "surfer boy" Scott Kendrick to head up the Nevada region, and kept Brett Todd in Fresno, right where he belonged, to restore order to a financially distressed, but victorious battlefield.

Backing up a bit, while all the bullshit was flying back and forth between Ernie and I over being allowed to regionalize the Group or not, Dave Hummel, my Tucson based Group Rental Manager (the guy who replaced Dick Jansen) took a Regional Vice President's position in Detroit. When the time came for Dave to make a decision, I recommended he take the promotion, saying, "Dave, at this point, I don't even know if I'll have a job much longer, let alone if this fucking Group will ever be regionalized."

He wisely bolted to Detroit. I liked Dave; he did a good job for me, and had that free-spirited, fun-loving attitude that the whole company seemed to have back in the '80s, but was slowly fading away as we neared a new millennium.

My relationship with my new Corporate Vice President seemed okay, but looking back on it, Tim Welsh was nowhere to be seen nor heard from when his successor, Rick Fish, was giving me my second and fatal dose of knife in back syndrome. Obviously, it would be rare for a corporate weasel to endanger their career by strongly supporting an original pay plan General Manager, when such action may bring them down as well.

Welsh, being a smart weasel, kept his mouth shut, and kept his job. He had already displayed his lack of courage at a Fall Officers Meeting when he steadfastly refused to correct a minor miscue by Andy Taylor, for fear that King Andrew would behead him. By the late '90s, fear of reprisal was permeating the ranks of corporate, especially amongst the likes of Welsh and his fellow weasels; as they stayed clear of even the slightest amount of controversy, scurrying to their offices in case of a sighting by anyone who might pose a threat to their job security.

I first got to know Tim in the early '90s when he was a Regional Vice President working under the Bill Hole Southern California dictatorship. Tim was a very young looking bald dude, who seemed to be a fun-loving, hilarious, and downright rambunctious guy; I soon found out that he blatantly cheated at golf more than anyone I ever knew; I also found out Tim was one of the cheapest individuals ever to walk the planet, but I've known lots of honorable tightwads who would never consider cheating to avoid paying a bet. Cheating took being a cheapskate to a whole new level; and as far as I'm concerned that level is pretty low.

Consequently, losing a bet didn't necessarily matter to Tim; he just wouldn't pay. He still owes me a hundred bucks on a basketball wager made several years ago, but I'll never see it.

Playing golf with Tim was actually quite amusing; he tried every ploy imaginable to throw his opponent off their game, and if that didn't work, he'd shave a stroke or two off his score at strategic moments to compensate. Since he was a pretty good golfer to begin with, the prospect of getting some of that money out of his fat wallet at the end of the round was challenging, but when successful, very rewarding and good for a laugh.

Darren Gottschalk, my recently acquired Tucson based RVP, was a good friend of Tim from their Southern California days, and witnessed some hilarious moments on the golf course when things just didn't go Tim's way.

The best story Darren told described a very stressed out Tim, faced with a mere "tap in" on the last hole to win a bunch of money, completely choked as Darren, taking a page out of Welsh's play book of dirty tricks, deliberately hovered ever so close to him while he tried to concentrate.

When the short putt lipped out, much to the delight of Gottschalk and company, an enraged Welsh took the putter that betrayed him and violently slammed the business end of the failed piece of equipment into the perfectly manicured, pristine and defenseless green, much like a crazed Jack Nicholson in "The Shining" causing mayhem with his ax.

As bedlam broke out, a grinning Gottschalk calmly extracted the putter left behind by a fuming Welsh, which was sticking out of the ground at a 45 degree angle; took a divot mender out of his pocket, and meticulously repaired the damage to the green as a very pissed off Tim, with his beet red bald head glowing like a neon light, stormed to the clubhouse. Darren then cleaned the head of the putter so thoroughly it looked brand new, and gave it back to its rightful owner, after Tim reluctantly opened his fat wallet and doled out some money; the dishonorable Mr. Welsh now had a bad case of the yips.

On the few occasions I played with Tim, his mood directly corresponded with his skill level during the round. Even if he happened to be teamed up with someone else, it really didn't matter if his partner had just birdied a hole to win it for the team; if Welsh bogeyed it, he'd be furious.

To avoid those nasty bogeys, whenever Tim would hit an errant shot to another county, somehow after a ten-minute search for the ball, he'd mysteriously "find" it, usually nestled in a nice spot, with a clean lie, and quite visible to anyone looking in that exact spot, just moments before; as we all had. On one such occasion when I knew he was cheating and he was getting ready to take his next shot, I yelled out to him, "So, you're dropping there, huh?" Very indignantly, he'd insist, "No, that's where I found it!"

"Really? Well, I guess it must've hit a tree, causing it to bounce a hundred yards right back to that nice little, unobstructed lie, which would allow you to save par if you can get it up and down from there, huh? But wait, I don't see any trees in the direction your ball was heading. Do you suppose it hit that house way over there; can you see it, on top of that mountain?"

Of course, the only reason I joke about Tim's questionable ethics is because I don't like cheaters; they may be likeable cheaters, but cheaters can never be trusted. I'd get a kick out of his antics; and he used to enjoy mine; but if you happen to be working under a guy who cheats at golf, or anything else for that matter, you know that weasel is not going to help you out when the rumblings of negative sentiment about you are coming down from above.

As Rick Fish quietly slithered into place as our new corpulent Corporate Vice President, while Tim Welsh and his fat wallet scurried away, the West Group was having its best year ever; I'd be celebrating my 25th year with the company, and felt like I was on top of the world.

Chapter 28
Backstabbing, Part II

believe it was May of '88 while in St Louis for only my second General Manager's meeting, Van Black, our amusing meeting coordinator, gathered the fifteen or so of us together to announce we were going to have our pictures taken. Nobody, including me, seemed too thrilled with this mundane activity, as we shuffled over to the area in the small building where we were having our little meeting, which served as the backdrop for our photo ops.

These pictures would then be placed in the company's old "image brochures", which were primarily used for recruiting purposes, to lure those young college graduates to hop on board the Enterprise express, where someday, they might make it big, like these assholes right here in this picture.

I always liked Van. He was the guy who drove me, my future ex-wife, Pam, and a few other fun-loving managers down to a bar somewhere in St Louis, where love would blossom for the two "love birds". For years, Van always would mention his role as "cupid" to me, until Pam and I were separated and he then developed amnesia.

As the camera crew made their entrance, I couldn't help but notice the female who seemed to be in charge of the operation; and neither could any of my gawking colleagues, for that matter. Old Van, that sly devil, arranged this entire activity with a company that employed a beautiful woman by the name of Ruth Guerri, who by some remarkable coincidence graced the cover of the July 1983 edition of Playboy Magazine; not to mention the center section as well.

For you Playboy trivia buffs, Ruth also made an appearance in the January 1979 edition, vying for the honor of becoming the 25th Anniversary Playmate. Although she wasn't chosen at that particular time, along with several other future centerfolds, Hef stayed in touch, did lunch, and offered her the Playmate spot a few years later.

Suddenly, in the presence of the very hot Miss July 1983, nobody was complaining about having to pose for pictures, and those smiles on our goofy faces were genuine.

A decade later, as I'm planning a little house warming party in Las Vegas to show off my new bachelor pad, one of our employee's husband; a frequently unemployed, although talented artist who I'd use from time to time to help out with stuff like that (primarily to help supplement his income to keep his wife from being a total bitch but it didn't work because they got divorced anyway), proudly announces to me, "Larry, a friend of mine is a friend of a guy who runs a modeling agency, and guess what?"

"You got me a date with one of the models? Thanks, man!" I knew that wasn't the case; I was just fucking with him.

"No, numb nuts; we're going to have like four or five of their models serving drinks for all your guests. Isn't that great?"

No doubt about it. I thought it was a great idea, as my mind was already conjuring up the prospects of finding one who was single, not dating anyone, and who would agree to dinner, dancing, and a movie, or something; with a guy like me. My heart soared, like eagle.

Nice try, Uncle Larry. These babes were either married dating somebody, or lying about it to avoid hurting the feelings of the old warrior, knowing that I would be a disgrace to my village if I were rejected in a shameful fashion.

It didn't matter; the hot girls were very nice, they were very professional, and very easily could've been centerfolds, had they so desired. I'm not sure if Hef ever offered them the gig, but none of them went in that direction.

As it turned out, the old warrior would hire them again for another party, just a few months later, and in the process, somehow became a disgrace to my village.

I didn't realize how scandalous this was until my new corporate spineless jellyfish told me so several months later, when an unhappy Albuquerque employee in the human resources department (Mark Tobiassen's region) complained about a promotion she was denied to work for Pam Nicholson at corporate, claiming she was unfairly rejected because Pam chose one of her old Southern California cronies instead.

While in the process of trying to squeeze as much money as possible out of the company to compensate her for the usual pain and suffering that naturally comes from the anguish of being discriminated against (she happened to be an Hispanic female, making her a double threat), she made a point of mentioning something extra special about me, which happened to be inaccurate, but Rick Fish thought he'd denounce me anyway as a disgrace to my village.

Trying to sound disappointed that a man of my stature with the company would do something so distasteful, he said, "Larry, she said you had this wild party at your house with these, uh, women, uh, and nobody knew why they were there, and, uh, it just seemed strange."

I tried to understand what seemed so strange. Was he saying that having women at my party made it look like I was not gay? Was I now the victim of discrimination, as well? Worse yet, was I really a disgrace to my village?

What really seemed strange to me was this corporate flunky would actually believe the validity of that statement, considering the person making it had a not so hidden agenda to accomplish. For good measure, she also claimed Mark Tobiassen, a soft-spoken family man who never even comes close to saying or doing anything even remotely inappropriate, had indeed done something inappropriate to be a disgrace to his village as well, according to this credible witness. A very flabbergasted Mark, looked at me and said, "I can't believe she would lie like that. I just can't believe it."

I just said, "Mark, at this point, nothing would surprise me. She's just throwing out as much shit as possible to see if it helps her get a little more money; you don't have a thing to worry about. Me on the other hand; holy shit, I've got some issues going on here."

Apparently concerned about the validity of her discrimination allegation, to avoid a probable lawsuit, corporate immediately negotiated a settlement without bothering to confer with Mark or I, beforehand. But this was West Group, not corporate, money they were throwing away, with absolutely no input from either of us; it was only after the fact that we were told by a stammering Rick Fish what had transpired on the conference call we were now engaged in, while Mark and I stared incredulously at each other, fuming over what we were hearing.

I realized at that moment, in December 1999, that the company I knew and loved had violated its most fundamental principle of conducting business. I had been stripped of whatever autonomy I once possessed, and in essence, was no longer a General Manager. I was still getting paid like one, and my staff still respected me, but without any real decision making authority, you're just a puppet flopping helplessly in whatever direction the corporate puppet master decides to pull you. For this particular puppet show, the puppet master flipped me completely upside down, and eighty thousand dollars spilled out of my puppet trousers, which was scooped up and given to this uh, chick.

Way before any of this became an issue, the Albuquerque employee in question, happened to be in Las Vegas during the weekend I hosted this "wild party". Knowing she was going to be in town that particular weekend, I invited her and her boyfriend to come over for the little shin dig; they did and strangely enough, seemed to have a wonderful time; but then months later made the insinuating "bitches and strippers and whores; oh my" type comment while strangely enough, trying to milk corporate for as much money as she could get. Hmm.

The fact that she trumped up the story to help her get money out of this paranoid company doesn't surprise me at all. The fact that my Corporate Vice President; the high level Officer who is supposed to be representing the company's best interests, somehow bought into this fairy tale, and now is scolding me about the fictitious crap she was dishing out as if it were completely true; that's what gets me.

But I suppose, that was the general idea; I was being "had" and the convenient allegation made it so easy to accomplish. The truth was inconsequential, as long as the story served its purpose, to undermine my authority, which was already fading away even before this bullshit.

This latest round of backstabbing was getting even more ridiculous than before; something I thought would never be possible. But it was happening, and my corporate backstabber wasn't really trying to hide the knife at all; he was sharpening it right in plain view in preparation for the final assault.

Backstabbing, Part II was in full swing.

Shortly after this trumped up scandal emerges, Fish slithers from his corporate command post to make his first Group visit to Las Vegas; his mission was quite simple; try to dig up some more dirt on me, and once again, the relevance of whatever he can dig up doesn't really matter; when he overhears a few employees playfully calling me "Uncle Larry", a ludicrously innocuous tradition that had been going on for so many years, suddenly making a bid deal out of that seemed quite silly. But that's exactly what happened.

The theme of this final assault now revolves around the general lack of respect I must have, and the logical place to begin is by lambasting a harmless, but apparently inappropriate nickname. Suddenly, "Uncle Larry" becomes synonymous with other notoriously bumbling "Uncles" over the years; forget the fact that these were fictitious characters.

My favorite analogy is George Bailey's Uncle Billy ("It's a Wonderful Life"), the dimwitted codger who screws up a bank transaction, causing George so much grief he nearly jumps off a bridge in total despair, only to be saved by George's Guardian Angel, Clarence; George comes out smelling like a rose, and Clarence gets his wings; at least that story had a happy Hollywood ending; isn't that right, Clarence?

With that plan of attack determined by the corporate hierarchy, the strategy now focused on completely inane topics like this, along with the fictitious wild parties hosted by the lewd and lascivious Uncle Larry, a person who clearly doesn't fit the required code of appropriate Enterprise Officer behavior.

While Rick was out for that little Group visit, realizing that an unfavorable shift in corporate sentiment towards me was well under way, I simply told him, "Rick, I've been around for a pretty long time, and I think I'm doing a pretty good job; but if guys like Andy or Don, don't feel I'm a valuable asset to the company, so be it, and I'll gladly step aside."

As I dropped this load off at McCarron International Airport for his trip back home, Fish quickly shook my hand, eased himself out of the passenger seat, reached for his brief case and carry on bag in the back seat, and with the half-assed obligatory final wave with his right fin, headed inside the terminal. Upon his arrival in St Louis, Fish would write a scathing memo to me, highlighted by the observation that it's practically impossible for anybody to respect a General Manager who allows himself to be called "Uncle Larry".

This would be my final visit from the corporate hierarchy.

As I pulled away from the curb and merged with the endless sea of vehicles leaving the airport, mostly taxis and limos, I couldn't help but think as I made my way back to the now relaxed atmosphere of my unpretentious administrative office, "I'm really getting tired of this bullshit."

Chapter 29

Losing My Autonomy And My Optimism

I was more than just a little weary of dealing with corporate type people after barely surviving the Ernie Badger assault. Tim Welsh seemed like a refreshing break from what I'd just been through, but I never trusted him. I liked him, though.

Rick Fish snuck in with no fan fare, and went largely unnoticed for several months, primarily because he never called, visited, or otherwise corresponded. I'd send my monthly recap memos to him and immediately jump on whatever project I needed to do, while Fish remained pleasantly invisible, swimming around corporate, trying to avoid the sharks.

As luck would have it, I suppose it must've been the kiss of death, but after returning from the Fall Officers Meeting clutching a President's Award as if it meant everything would now be perfect from now on, all hell breaks loose in Las Vegas.

That didn't take long. I suppose reality is more interesting, anyway.

A company has just burned us for fifty grand in uncollectable rental charges, and in the heat of the moment, Mike Andera and I are both on the verge of resigning because we're both taking opposite sides of the issue. We would later come to terms with that disagreement, but at the time everything is unfolding, it looked like we'd never be able to work together, so I seriously thought about stepping aside right then and there because he was young and needed to make more money and stuff, and I was just getting sick and tired of the bullshit.

Naturally, I call Fish to alert him of the crisis, and over the phone he's telling me not to worry; these things happen; and all that positive crap you hear from corporate people while they're thinking, "If this guy went away, I'd be a hero, and everybody would like me." The seed for the next round of backstabbing had been planted.

Gradually, the furor in Las Vegas dies down a bit, the bad debt is written off, and one area manager is fired; now it's time for another fiasco; this time in the car sales department, and just in time for the holidays.

One fine December day, something unscrupulous in the car sales department is brought to my attention, and to complicate matters even more, this activity also involves the San Francisco Group. To put it succinctly, the two Group Car Sales managers are in cahoots in this bad behavior.

After calling Fish to fill him in on the situation, and that I've decided to fire my guy, he tells me to hold off until he has the chance to talk to Bob Caspar, San Francisco's General Manager. After that conversation takes place, and Bob decides to take similar action, I'm finally allowed to take the appropriate action; but it was never clear to me why I needed clearance from above to begin with.

Ironically, thanks to the careful and meticulous detective work performed by our Group employees, Brian Patch and John Wilmer, the problem is identified and resolved. San Francisco never had a clue anything unethical was going on right under their noses, so when the West Group makes the discovery, I told my guys I thought they were heroes even though it didn't seem like corporate shared that sentiment; or if they did, they didn't want anybody to know.

While all this fuss was going on, corporate was busy handling the discrimination allegation from our Albuquerque human resources liar, and promptly throws her a bunch of money (West Group money) to appease her; without bothering to consult me or Mark Tobiassen beforehand; an act that was a cardinal sin, in a previous era.

The way things were playing out, as the trend of my fading autonomy continued, I lost the optimism I had just a couple of months prior, when I triumphantly returned from the Washington DC Fall Officers Meeting, with a nice President's Award souvenir; but that's all it really was.

The harsh reality of business was getting harsher each passing day; and as the world is preparing for the big event; a new millennium; 010100; I decide to hold another "wild" party at my house to celebrate what would turn out to be the final year of my Enterprise career.

The countdown to 010101 had begun.

Chapter 30

The Issue Would Finally Be Addressed

After the predominantly silent visit from Rick Fish, his subsequent scathing "Uncle Larry can't possibly be respected" memo to me, and my rebuttal, which he admitted "addressed all major concerns", the next three months go by with little consequence, although the uneasy feeling I have about the discussions going on behind closed doors at 600 Corporate Park Drive persists.

In May, I attend my final spring meeting in St Louis, and decide, what the fuck, I'm going to have a carefree attitude the entire time, not really worrying about the furor that may be going on from the powers above me. By this time, I had already heard from several different sources attending the recently concluded rental managers meeting in Orlando, that I'd better start cleaning out my office; I had fallen from that high spot off the company ladder with nothing to grab onto on the way down, and no net to prevent the inevitable and fatal, hard landing.

I had a very simple approach to rumors; especially rumors about me. I just went about my business and let everybody else do the speculating. The way I saw it, the last four years of high income employment were almost a gift; I very easily could've been whacked in '96; but I not only survived, I thrived. If I was considered to be an unacceptable Officer for the company in 2000; so be it; just show me where to sign and I'll see y'all later.

When the meetings began, I felt a bit detached already, sensing the corporate tension surrounding me, but indifferent to their plans. I had almost become an impartial observer of my own career; I had already achieved more than I thought possible; escaping the Ernie Badger ordeal with, no doubt, a tarnished reputation with the hierarchy; but after finally being allowed to regionalize the Group, kept posting more impressive results with each subsequent fiscal year.

After walking away with a President's Award, just seven months prior, and well on our way to an even stronger fiscal year (each fiscal year ends on July 31), on the surface, all appeared well in the Wild, Wild West Group. As I greeted some of my long-time colleagues; Dick Jansen, Tony Moist, Tom Tobin, Robert Ward, and my original "new hire" as I opened the Phoenix Group back in 1981, Jim Loomer; I felt a sense of pride from my role in helping these guys become successful General Managers.

The measure of one's personal success quite often is gauged by the success others achieve, aided by your guidance and support. In essence, that's what gave me the most satisfaction about my contribution to the company; in my mind, that was my simple legacy, not being regarded as "the company funny man", as the bland company newsletter (cleverly called "free Enterprise") of the humorless corporation would later dub me, in its tribute to the soon to be retiring, Uncle Larry.

At the same time, I thought about some of my old buddies who preceded me in becoming General Managers; guys like Dave Willey and Dick Rush, whose vehemence at the preposterous notion prohibiting "rental only" management from reaching "Level 4" had merit, as a reluctant company would agree; resulting in a new generation of management talent that was driven by the upstart and restless rental division.

As I mingled with the other General Managers and corporate Officers at what would prove to be my final spring General Managers meeting; a bunch of old St Louis natives such as myself, Stan Mann, Ed Forbusch, Dennis Slavik, Dennis Reinhardt, John Ebeling, Bob Klaskin, Ed McCarty, Steve Adams, Bruce Kruenegel, Roger Price, John O'Connell, Mark Miller, Bill Hole, Pam Nicholson, Ernie Badger, Don Ross, and of course Andy Taylor himself, the President of this large corporation; in addition to Andy's dad, Jack; all of us owed a debt of gratitude to both Wayne Kaufmann and Doug Brown for helping pave the way for our success.

Strangely, this Enterprise "odd couple" who seemed to be completely opposite from the other; one a home-spun, farting, Army veteran; a country boy with only a high school diploma but lots of business savvy, bred strictly in rental, and the other a dynamic, chain-smoking, smooth talking Jewish kid from Ladue (a wealthy St Louis suburb), who worked his way up the company ladder through the leasing department; who routinely mixed profanity in with his conversations, the way normal people should talk; who coined one of my favorite expressions, "a thousand give a shits".

This pair of rivals who were really cohorts, were the root of everything good that would happen with Executive Leasing/Enterprise Leasing/ Enterprise Rent-a-Car; and the chances that any of the thousands of employees working for this company today have ever heard of them are, sadly, remote.

Certainly, both Brown and Kaufmann have been mentioned in previous corporate authorized, coffee table books that seldom actually get "read" by anyone, including the current hard working employees of Enterprise Rent-a-Car, who many disgruntled segments of that group derisively refer to themselves as "E-tards"; their humorous way of dealing with the craziness of the business and the questionable management tactics of their immediate supervisors; and if both Doug and Wayne were still with the company, they'd find a way to reassure the vast majority of any disillusioned employees that things would work out just fine in the long run; so stop that fucking bitching and moaning, okay?

The overall meeting was otherwise forgettable for me, with the exception of some of the humorous moments that always seemed to spontaneously occur, when least expected.

During one of the general sessions, my favorite corporate agitator, Ernie Badger was called upon to give a presentation about business ethics, dealing with security issues, employee theft and dishonesty, and so on. As the pompous self appointed guardian of administrative and fiduciary propriety, it seemed appropriate that he'd be the one called upon to lecture everybody in his usual stern, intimidating, and irritating tone.

For some reason, Ernie decided to place his mouth right on top of the microphone, which not only looked gross, it created a Darth Vader like tone, only much louder. Speaking very loudly, as if he had no microphone at all, it seemed he wanted to make sure he could be heard from, let's say, the centerfield bleachers to home plate at a typical major league ballpark. You could imagine the conversation that would take place at home plate between the batter, the catcher and the umpire during any break in the action.

"Do you hear that asshole out there in the bleachers?"

"Yeah, he's been driving me crazy all day long. He won't shut the fuck up."

"Well, I'll tell you what; you'd better swing at anything even close to the plate because it's going to be a strike. We've got to get this game over real quick because I can't take much more of this shit. Now, let the goddamned force be with you and play ball!"

So there we sat while Darth Vader sternly admonished us for something we weren't doing anyway. It was very strange, and really, quite hilarious; as soon as he blasted his first word, it seemed like the entire group of shocked managers had been rear ended by a Budweiser beer truck. There may have been a few cases of whiplash as heads snapped backwards throughout the stunned gathering. Humorous murmurs persisted while the amplified tirade relentlessly continued.

Ernie was either oblivious to the decibel level he was creating, or thought the impact of his words being belted in such deafening tones sounded ominous and lord knows he loved to intimidate whenever possible by, I suppose, trying to sound like the lord.

Eventually, his presentation came to a merciful conclusion, as I removed my index fingers from both ear canals, pleased that I had successfully avoided any permanent hearing loss, and pleased that I had accomplished that feat so irreverently.

A bit later on in the day, during a rousing break out session, people were still chuckling about the loudest speech ever given in Enterprise history, and Ernie's name jokingly came up pertaining to something or other; I don't recall; but I immediately launched into an impromptu impersonation of Ernie, which prior to this moment, I'd never even considered it as part of my repertoire, but I nailed it perfectly, cupping my hands in front of my mouth to enhance the volume, I sarcastically bellowed, "Can you hear me now?" Unbelievably, it sounded exactly like Ernie who always seemed to be heard wherever he went, even when you really didn't want to hear him at all.

The room roared in raucous laughter; the good old Enterprise guffaw, and I immediately knew my impersonation of the lord, Ernie Badger might well be considered sac-religious by the high papal authority of corporate sanctity, but what the hell; I just couldn't resist that temptation; even with my current preacher, Rick Fish floating right next to me; although he appeared to be amused by it all; but if not, a thousand give a shits.

That may have been the high point of my career of irreverence, although it didn't even cross mind at the time; I was just looking for a pitch I could handle; got a hanging curve and knew it was gone as soon as I hit it. As I rounded the bases, I thought to myself, "Gee,

I'm a lucky stiff."

Just a couple of months earlier, Ernie and a bunch of Enterprise cronies came to Las Vegas for a couple of days to play a little golf and do a little gambling. The weather was horrible and the one round I attempt to play with these guys was set up strategically to have me riding in the same cart with Ernie. Dennis Reinhardt, the guy I was commiserating with in the hotel bar about Ernie's torturous management style, prior to the '96 Fall Officers meeting, very quickly switched his bag from Ernie's cart to Bruce McKee's (one of the funniest guys I've ever known) and before I could do anything about it, had my bag in his vacated spot.

I looked at him with mock disdain, while he was smugly grinning, and said, "Thanks a lot, bones." "No problem, Lars."

For me, using the horrible weather and a the fact that I actually had to like, go to work and everything, as an excuse, I bolt after nine hellish holes.

I met the guys later that evening for dinner at the Palms Restaurant, one of my favorite hang outs, and we're all in a jovial mood as each new bottle of Merlot is dispensed. I plopped myself between Ernie Badger and Tampa's General Manager, Dennis Slavik, who happened to be my old boss when I was running the Clayton branch back in '80-81. I had respect for Dennis, as I had lost the edge of thinking all leasing guys were assholes; and he told me shortly before I got the promotion to Phoenix, that I was "sitting in a tall saddle" as the top rental manager in St Louis; and that made me feel like Clint Eastwood, for sure.

Dennis, who was sitting on my left, quietly confided in me that he would be retiring soon, and asked me how much longer I thought I'd be hanging in there before calling it quits. I just said, "Dennis, it's hard to say; I'm taking it month by month, but don't be surprised if I join you pretty soon; the bullshit's getting harder to deal with almost every day."

Dennis, who always sounded like a radio talk show host, with his deep voice, and cool delivery; whatever he said, sounded like he was always in complete control; he just gave a wry smile, and speaking in a very low tone, out of the corner of his mouth said, "You got that right, pal."

To my right was the relentless Ernie, who was engaged in conversation with guys like Ira Robb, who hadn't made it official yet, but he would be retiring at the end of the year, as well; Dennis Reinhardt, who still had a few years left in Atlanta; Roger Price, who would hang in there a little longer himself; as well as the hilarious Bruce McKee, who would last seemingly forever.

After a while, Ernie turned his head in my direction, and we began a little good-natured banter about nothing in particular, as we tried to put aside the mutual animosity of days gone by. Holding grudges never accomplished much as far as I could tell, but having a little fun with them was an entirely different matter.

Now that Ernie theoretically had no influence on my career, I just couldn't resist goading him on, "Ernie, remember that stable of women that you thought I had a few years ago? Well, I've got one now!"

As I laughed that mock Enterprise guffaw, the forced laugh that just doesn't sound genuine, a laugh that I'd heard hundreds of times before at various Enterprise meetings, I assured him I was only kidding. Ernie, gave me a vacant smile, not really sure if I was indeed only kidding, or if I had that stable somewhere; his confused look somehow pleased me.

I knew my career was winding down, but I certainly never lost any sleep worrying about that or the fact that having a stable of women was probably never going to happen; I was prepared to handle whatever came my way, because I knew I had accomplished a lot for a pretty long time, had a positive impact on a lot of people I worked with over the years, and was financially secure.

The phone call finally came on June 29, 2000.

It seemed so ironic that three separate phone calls would be so memorable to me, yet the only one I could remember the exact date, was the last one. The first, from Wayne Kaufmann, would send me to Phoenix; the second from Doug Brown, would make me a General Manager; and the third, from Rick Fish, of all people, would send me packing. I suppose when your career is rising, you remember the calls but don't pay much attention to the exact dates the calls were made; you just assume things will keep moving forward, forever.

That second phone call, from Doug Brown, also included special guest appearances from Don Ross and the President himself, Andy Taylor.

This third phone call was a solo job; Fish was on his own; Ross and Taylor were gone, on other assignments.

The day seemed innocent enough, although I had a little voice mail from Fish, asking me to call. Usually a call from your Corporate Vice President meant something had gone wrong somewhere; but this time, I had a feeling that it was going to be more serious than a pissed off customer in Bakersfield.

Apparently, my return phone call to Rick caught him off guard, because rather than talk to me at the particular moment he asked if I'd read his inter-company e-mail. When I said I hadn't, he said, "Well, call me back after you've read it."

Since he was completely devoid of a personality (and possibly, a spine) and therefore any sense of humor whatsoever, I realized this was no gag. Still, just to make sure what I heard was correct, I restated what I thought he said.

"In other words, Rick; you want me to hang up; read a note that you sent me; and then call you back? Okay, I'll talk to you soon."

This reminded me of the Three Stooges episode where an irritated

Moe, for some unknown reason, slaps a sleeping Curly in the face, telling him "Wake up and go to sleep!"

My career had just reached a new low. It had become a Three Stooges episode.

I knew this milquetoast hated confrontation; in fact, during his Group visit to Las Vegas the prior February, he admitted he was intimidated by Pam Nicholson, the highest ranking female corporate officer in company history (Rick's boss), and apparently a person who intimidates a milquetoast like this one. I didn't feel intimidated by her, and in fact, I wasn't particularly impressed with her the first time I had any sort of business dealings with her.

Why, I remember it almost as if it were yesterday, or the day before yesterday; yes, that's how well I remember it.

I think it was in 1992, when Dick Jansen and I were negotiating a deal with Jim Click, a big-time Ford dealer in Tucson. Jim was a likeable character; he was a brash, no nonsense, fun-loving guy from Oklahoma who loved to play golf, and enjoyed playing games with nervous people who were trying to get some business from him.

At the time, Pam was a nervous Regional Vice President in Southern California, and Jim had a dealership in Orange County that could send her a ton of business, if collectively, Enterprise did everything Jim wanted.

This was one of those deals that would be a slam-dunk and while Dick and I joked with each other and with Jim, poor Pam sat there looking dazed and confused. When she spoke, she sounded like she was giving a canned presentation for Amway or something.
Every word out of her mouth sounded like she was nervously reading a script, instead of simply having a business discussion.

Jim was obviously having fun with the situation; he already knew Dick and I, and in fact had played golf with us on a couple of occasions prior to this meeting, and we'd established a good rapport.

All we needed to do was finalize a couple of loose ends and we'd be in business.

As we bantered back and forth, finally our mission was accomplished; Jim suddenly grinned and hollered out with his classic Oklahoma twang, "Hell, you guys are great! We got ourselves a deal!"

Afterwards, a very relieved Pam Nicholson, knowing that she could return to Southern California with good news for her boss, Bill Hole; relaxed and started kidding around with us a little bit. She seemed like a nice young lady once she stopped worrying about things.

Of course, Pam went on to much bigger things than I would ever accomplish, as she was a Corporate Vice President for a while, then took over the New York Group for a while, before going back to corporate as the number three guy for a while.

In the summer of 2008, Pam Nicholson became the number two guy, becoming President of the company Jack built. Andy Taylor, still the number one guy, as "Chairman and Chief Executive Officer", announcing this significant promotion in the company's bland newsletter, proudly observed, "There is no better example of our promote-from-within business model at work."

I suppose that promote-from-within business model was built after the Lu Slips Tucson debacle, huh, Andy?

Sadly, the real number one guy, Jack Taylor, at the age of 86, is pretty much out of the picture these days, and the aging Don Ross, is now content to be serving in a "supporting mode" for the newly appointed President.

Ironically, I may have played some role in Pam Nicholson's remarkable success. When I left the St Louis Group in May of 1981 to open Phoenix, somebody had to fill the void at the Clayton office; and that was accomplished with Ed Forbush making a good lateral move to take over my old branch (Ed later became General Manager of the Denver Group).

The trickle down effect inevitably created the need to hire another brand new management trainee; and sure enough, that person just happened to be the future President, Pam Nicholson. Arguably, Pam probably would've landed at Enterprise sooner or later, but who knows; maybe she would've gone on to work at someplace like Georgia Pacific instead, if I had hung around St Louis a while longer; and maybe she wouldn't have been laid off, since they were making money by that time. Maybe she would've become a district sales manager or something.

Oh well; towards the end of my career I knew the future President didn't particularly care for me, but it was no big deal; I didn't particularly care for her by that time, either; she always seemed too stressed out; I probably seemed too irreverent. Since she was, like, the number three guy and moving upwards, I never stood a chance of surviving this stressed out environment very long.

Some casual observers had noticed that I was the only Officer receiving a President's Award at the Fall Officers Meeting in '99, who didn't hug her as I accepted my final plaque. Fuck, the last thing either of us wanted to do at that moment was hug each other. I didn't hug Andy or Don so was the rationale for hugging Pam based on the fact that she's a chick?

I shook their hands, smiled, accepted the Award, posed for the obligatory photo op, jumped off the podium, and sprinted back to my seat. I can't be certain, but I think I may have set a new Enterprise President's Award acceptance land speed record. I got a great break right out of the starting blocks, as soon as I heard, "Larry", I figured it was me; I just took a direct route to the podium, got there in no time at all, and thanks to not hugging anybody, got a quick return, with no wasted motion, and was right back in my seat, just like that. Years of training really paid off for me there.

A smiling Mike Andera, who was now my Vice President of Finance, seemed to get a kick out of the routine, and I gave him the knowing smile right back, while blowing out a sigh of relief; or maybe I was just a little bit out of shape.

One of the corporate good guys, Wayne Kaufmann's replacement, Jeff Brummet, who was around when I gave my big speech heard 'round the Enterprise world way back in '83, bravely saluted me during my dash, shouting "Go Pedro!" That brought a smile to my face, but it was apparent this little company inside joke was becoming a distant memory by the end of the '90s, as the majority of that crowd didn't get it.

Unbeknownst to me, a new Enterprise era had arrived; and this new breed of Officers felt compelled to hug that number three guy, Pam Nicholson, if they were chosen to receive a President's Award; it was indeed true; every other recipient (I'm guessing about twenty or so huggers) gave Pam a big old hug while up on that podium, which I think was my key to getting the land speed record; but again, I can't really prove it. In those days, there were no fancy stopwatches or video.

I recall being in some little meeting (appropriately called a "mini GM meeting") with Pam and some other General Managers, and she didn't like an answer I gave to some hypothetical business question. Rather than simply state that she didn't agree with me, she thought it would be fun to treat me like a 4th grader who was the classroom idiot. She first stared at me incredulously, and then asked the rest of the classroom, "Well, does anybody agree with Larry?"

Nobody raised a hand, which I thought was rather amusing since I knew most of those assholes, who were now looking in other directions when I tried to make eye contact, did in fact, agree with me because we talked about it right before the oral examination; meanwhile, I looked back up at a glaring Pam, expecting the future President to slam a dunce cap on my head, at any moment.

Enough reminiscing; after reading the message Fish sent, which absolutely had to be read before he would converse with me, said something to the effect, "As we previously discussed, if your performance indicates to Andy or Don that you should retire, we would need to address that issue."

That was an interesting way to put it, I thought. My "performance", in terms of the measurable core areas of the company, outperformed roughly, 75% of the other Groups.

After hanging up, reading that blurb, and calling him back in stooge-like fashion to address that issue, Rick was now as prepared to deal with me as he was going to get, saying something like, "Uh, we think you should retire, because, uh, you didn't do a very good job at the, uh, San Diego meeting."

"Really? Andy and Don want me to go because I didn't do a very good job as a break out leader in San Diego. That's it?"

Fish mumbled something vague, but again, that word " performance" was mixed into his closing argument, as his voice trailed off; he really needed to hang up now, because he had to get home, and pack for a two week vacation he would be taking the very next day; it was quite obvious, he was under a lot of pressure to get this issue finally addressed before he could get out of town.

After concluding the conversation and hoping he and his family had a good time at Wally World, I thought I'd shoot Rick a quick little inter-company e-mail about my overall "performance" as a General Manager. After coming off a President's Award winning fiscal year, the current fiscal year, which had just one more month to complete, was even better.

Roughly speaking, the artist formerly known as Uncle Larry was outperforming three out of four General Managers in the entire company. Since I wasn't sure if Rick would still be in the office after I sent this instant message, I decided to deliver a carbon copy to Don Ross, as well.

Don's terse reply stated it really wasn't a question of performance, per se. Rather, it had more to do with issues concerning "culture, example, and philosophy." My personal life, which had been under attack since the Ernie "Darth Vader" Badger days, and continued with Rick Fish's weak accusations of wild parties and debauchery, now was vaguely tied in with nice sounding business jargon concerning my deficiencies in "culture, example, and philosophy". It still sounded like bullshit to me.

In reality, although my straightforward and irreverent management style of giving my managers a good deal of autonomy, while projecting a friendly, approachable persona to the young trainees in the trenches, was disliked by the corporate hierarchy, as they slowly drained me of the autonomy I once took for granted; I've got to believe my projected income for the very next fiscal year, somewhere in the irreverent neighborhood of $6 million, was on top of the list for taking the necessary action.

Certainly, the prospect of me, of all people, making that kind of money was more than the corporate hierarchy could now bear; but how could they possibly admit that? It just wouldn't fit their image; so they decided to go with the "culture, example, philosophy" route; it had a good ring to it. I fully understood the business realities, which this corporation never acknowledged in a straightforward manner.

Disillusioned, yet still proud of what I'd accomplished after a wild twenty-six year run, it was indeed time to go; the convenient excuses were unnecessary.

Chapter 31
No Regrets

At the conclusion of that brief phone call with Rick Fish, not much is resolved logistically speaking. It would take a couple of weeks to work out the details since he was about to embark on his well-deserved vacation.

Hanging up the phone after that bizarre conversation, and sending my parting thoughts to Rick and Don Ross about my "performance" as a General Manager, in an inter-company e-mail, I had one of the strangest feelings I'd ever had in my life.

Realizing the inevitable had just taken place, the rush of emotion that twenty-six years of working for this one company produced overwhelmed me, as I had to sit back and reflect on things a bit.

The strange feeling I had wasn't shock; it wasn't dismay; it wasn't elation; and even though I felt relieved about the prospect of not having to deal with a corporate bureaucracy any more, I felt strangely detached, because it also meant I wouldn't be a part of the Group I came to love, from top to bottom.

Yes, it was most definitely weird. I decided I'd better get drunk that night.

Other than Mike Andera, who by this time I'd promoted to Vice President of Finance and a couple of other confidants, I keep all this to myself for a while. Mike wasn't happy about this development; his career, which was sailing right along quite smoothly, now was uncertain. He didn't want to go to corporate, but eventually, that's where he had to go, at least for a little while; from there, he sailed the Atlantic and wound up working for Enterprise in London town. I liked Mike; he wasn't afraid to disagree with me, and when he did, we got through it still respecting each other.

When he came on board, in late '96, we discussed a lot of philosophical business things, because that's what business people do sometimes; he wanted to get to what the Enterprise people call "Level 4"; that makes you an Officer of the company and you get to go to the big Fall Officers Meeting where spouses are welcome but if you don't have one, be prepared to be an outcast if you are separated or divorced because most of the Officers are happily married; but as a consolation, maybe you can round up a stable of women to have on the side.

Tim Welsh was still my Corporate Vice President when he approved my decision to promote Mike to the Vice President of Finance position. Usually not known for making a big deal out of things, I decided to make this a big surprise announcement with all the Regional Vice Presidents in attendance at a dinner meeting we were having at the Inn at Spanish Bay, in the Monterey Peninsula. We didn't normally have meetings there, but this was some sort of quarterly meeting thing and it was so fucking hot in Las Vegas we thought a nice, cooler climate would help our brains from becoming even more damaged; so now the stage is set for bumbling Uncle Larry to blow the simple toast I had planned.

What I had planned on saying went something like this, as I dramatically stood up and raised my glass of Merlot: "Here's to Mike Andera; our new Vice President of Finance!" At that point, I suppose everybody would've applauded, while shouting "Hip, hip, hooray!" Then, boldly, after an emotional but manly hug of Mike, we all would've started singing, "For He's a Jolly Good Fellow", and the entire hotel restaurant would've spontaneously joined in and started dancing in perfectly choreographed unison; and in the midst of all the revelry, with bag pipes now wailing away, I would've turned to the camera, cocked my right eyebrow, smiled, and winked a knowing wink. Fade to black.

In reality, what happened was I dramatically stood up and raised my glass of Merlot, which in turn shocked the shit out of everybody, causing me to be distracted, whereupon I forgot my very complicated toast. I think I stammered something like, "Here's to Mike Andera, who's now, uh, something like a level four, uh, Mike; help me out here! What's your new title going to be?"

I'll never forget the look of absolute, incredulous shock that Mike had on his face while I was trying to stammer through this wonderfully staged event. For a moment, he had no idea what the fuck I was doing, and for that matter nobody, including myself knew what was going on. Then, when he saw the pleading look on my face and heard "level four" he knew he'd made it. His wife, Susan, was there to share the moment, which was totally blown by me, but in all the hilarity, turned out pretty cool. I'm glad my mind went blank and I screwed up the toast; it would've been boring to do it right. Isn't that right, Clarence?

At Mike's first big Fall Officers Meeting, Andy Taylor, during his welcoming speech the first night of the festivities, dutifully calls out the names of the new Officers in attendance, a nice tradition to make the rookies feel welcome; unfortunately for Mike, Andy had his name wrong; and that will happen from time to time; so instead of saying "Andera", Andy called him "Andrea" (a chick's name); which of course is no big deal, but it's something that very tactfully should've been corrected.

When Tim Welsh came over later on to congratulate Mike, I casually mentioned that he tell Andy what Mike's last name is, so he can make the correction the next time he speaks. Welsh looked at me like I was asking him to punch Andy in the face, and said, "Hell, no; do you think I'm crazy? You tell him!"

Had I really thought nobody at corporate would have the balls to tell Andy something so innocuous, I would have approached Andy with it right then and there. Incredibly, no one did have the balls to dare correct the mad tyrant, known as Andrew Taylor, the Career Slayer.

I think the conversation would've been hysterical, reminiscent of dialogue from the great big business spoofing movie, "Office Space":

"Hey, Andy; what's happening? Uh, yeah, Andy; I just wanted to let you know Mike's last name actually is Andera, not Andrea; FYI; yeah, so if you could get it right in front of all those Officers and their, uh, spouses that would be great; yeah, it's spelled A-N-D-E-R-A; as in "how dare" you get my name wrong; yeah, thanks."

Uh, yeah; apparently, timid Tim and his other weasel associates at corporate feared that Andy would fly into a tyrannical rage, screaming, "How dare you correct me! You're fired, whatever your name is!"

I found it hard to believe they feared this man who I always regarded as straight forward, unpretentious; and would certainly take no offense about being notified that either a typographical error or dyslexia had caused him to mispronounce someone's name.

The funny thing was, Jack Taylor himself often had difficultly remembering names, and used to call everybody "Sport". The first time he actually remembered my name, and called me "Larry Underwood" at a rental managers meeting in 1981, I nearly fell out of my chair; I felt I'd finally arrived.

Another year passes, and I'm getting ready to give my little farewell speech, and it's already been finalized that Mike is going to work at corporate, ironically, directly reporting to Andy Taylor, after I've retired.

Again, as Andy's doing his usual welcoming speech, he makes the special announcement that Mike "Andrea" is coming to corporate to work directly under him, not only blowing the name for two consecutive speeches; but blowing the name of a guy who would be reporting directly to President What's His Name.

I look over at Mike and he's got that same sheepish grin he had last year, as if to say, "Oh, well."

Then he saw the look on my face and immediately starts shaking his head, as if to say, "Please, don't!" I'm smiling with the look of "Oh yes I will; uh, yeah."

Somewhere along the line, while I'm wrapping up my farewell gibberish to the faithful gathering, and Andy's nervously pacing behind me, I decide the time was right to finally take care of this terrifyingly and extremely delicate issue right then and there.

Turning around to make sure I had his attention, which I did, in a very matter of fact way, say, "Oh, by the way, Andy, it's Mike Andera, not Andrea; okay?" I really thought it would be nice if Andy knew his new right hand man's name, just in case it came in, uh, handy some day; yeah.

By that time, it had long been apparent to me that fear was permeating the ranks of corporate and the upper management teams in the field. I'm afraid I was getting sick of that shit.

Meanwhile, back at the whacking, I figured I'd tell the rest of the crew the news about my pending fate at an upcoming quarterly meeting we were having in Lake Tahoe. The first day up there we had a little lunch and played some golf, and I kept unusually quiet, especially since it was my fucking 48th birthday. I think the guys thought I was a little morose because I was getting so old. I was just contemplating my life.

The next day was the meeting day, and the first thing out of my mouth is "Guys, I'm not sure when it's going to be official, but I'm leaving the company." Kendrick starts snickering because he thinks I'm kidding, but I look at him and say, "I'm serious, Scott. I'm going to be meeting with Rick Fish next week sometime and I'll be able to give you more information, but I'm 99% sure I'm out of here."

Actually, the way things played out surprised me. After meeting with Fish for an hour or so, he says he's got to confer with Don Ross, and in turn, Rick would call me back to give me a definite date to mark on my calendar as a reminder that I don't have to go to work anymore. Usually, when a General Manager retires, it's pretty much instantaneous.

They let me be a lame duck through the end of the year; and that was pretty cool. My official retirement date would be January 1, 2001; or as I referred to it: "010101"

There was still quite a bit of legal verbiage to wade through before the official announcement could be made to the rest of the company, and that happened the latter part of August.

Andy Taylor, the guy who told me to get a sun tan, wear nicer suits, apologized to me for sticking me with his cousin Pam as my first assistant in Phoenix, and now is so feared at corporate that nobody would ever dare correct him, sent out the notice to the rest of the Enterprise world announcing my retirement at the end of the year, but reassuring everybody that they could all say goodbye to me at the upcoming Fall Officers Meeting. So now I still had to go to that goddamned meeting.

After twenty-six years with Enterprise, I had accomplished more than I dreamed possible, and I felt proud to have been a part of an entrepreneurial company that grew to dominate a very competitive industry. It was a wonderful ride, and I enjoyed every minute of it; but now it was time to go; with absolutely no regrets.

Chapter 32

A Mystifying Final Trip To St Louis

During the entire process of working out the logistics of my imminent departure from the company, I never had a single conversation with Andy Taylor or Don Ross. I had a great deal of respect for both gentlemen, and I was actually looking forward to visiting with them on my upcoming trip to St Louis in late August to sign off on the separation agreement. The document had to be notarized there, and I assumed a company noted for their class, would show some when I came to town.

Throughout the entire process, I believe I acted in an appropriately business like and amiable manner, and in fact, Don at one point in the negotiations acknowledged that fact in a brief note and thanked me for being so cooperative or whatever; I don't recall the exact words, but it sounded something along those lines. However, it was quite true; I was handling the process in a professional, business like manner, since after all that was in my job description.

I put aside the disappointment I felt when Don sent me the "culture, example, philosophy" note because nothing was going to change that sentiment; it was time to move on to the next step, and that would entail flying to St Louis to complete the document that would make me an ex-employee.

I never heard a word from Andy during that time, but I suppose that was not out of the ordinary with all the rigors of being the head-honcho of such a huge enterprise that Enterprise was. Then I thought this was a far cry from 1976 when Andy gave me that little pep talk when I got promoted to branch rental manager; or 1982, when Andy flew out from St Louis to apologize to me in Phoenix for sticking his cousin with me.

I arrived in St Louis the afternoon before my scheduled notarization process, and checked in to the Ritz Carlton, which was maybe a couple of miles from the big office. I was prepared to make that drive to 600 Corporate Park Drive, as soon as I heard from Rick, that everything was ready to go. I simply wanted to take care of the business at hand, and hopefully get the chance to visit with Andy Taylor and Don Ross to thank them for helping me in my career, and one that I considered fairly successful.

I suppose the corporate brain trust wanted no part of me wandering through their offices, and possibly being disruptive; I don't know. I do know that Fish told me to stay put, and that he and his notary would be down in a jiffy to handle things, over breakfast.

After the contract is finalized; only then does Rick indicate I would be an unwelcome sight at the corporate headquarters, as he snatched up the paperwork, and without even looking at me, just said, "Thanks, that'll do it. Have a good trip home."

I was taken aback to say the least. "You mean I won't be seeing Andy or Don?"

"No; Andy's out of town, and Don's too busy" as Fish was stuffing his briefcase with his copy of that notarized agreement.

At that point, I felt very insignificant; I was very tidily disposed of by one of their underlings, and in my attempt to make this as pleasant as humanly possible, I'm shot down by indifference; if that's how the company reflects its own "culture, example, and philosophy", then Don was absolutely correct in telling me I don't fit in.

The Fall Officers Meeting was coming up in a couple of months, and I was seriously thinking my best bet would be to skip it; as I became amused with my own irony, "What are they going to do if I blow this meeting off; fire me?"

Several weeks go by, and still no word from either top company executive, which again, seemed to be a classless way of dealing with someone who made some decent contributions to the overall success of the company.

As if on cue, both Andy and then Don finally make the dreaded phone calls to me, convincing me to give a little farewell speech at the big meeting. I thought about Andy's dad, Jack; and how it would be nice to pay tribute to him, in my own way, without bothering to prepare a formal speech; just let whatever I felt, flow through that microphone and confuse the hell out of the majority of the attendees not accustomed to seeing Uncle Larry's improvisational approach to giving speeches.

Graciously, I agreed to go, what the fuck.

Coincidentally, the two guys who launched the massive Southern California empire, none other than Bill Hole and Ira Robb, were also retiring, and in attendance; so this particular Fall Officers Meeting figured to be quite interesting, as two of the smartest guys I ever knew with Enterprise were going to be giving their farewell speeches along with little old me.

The only "no shows" of the Officers who were sliding out the door were Dennis Slavik; the guy who had confided in me early in the year that he would be retiring; and Rick Snyder, a guy who rose to the top of the fleet services ranks in the entire company, and coincidentally was a lease salesman at my original office when I was the number three guy; they had sense enough to stay away from that last dog and pony show.

Out of that quintet of Enterprise old guard millionaires, I was probably the pauper in the group. I assumed those other guys were averaging well over $10 million annually, so this year had to be a record breaking cost cutting Fall Officers send off, to be sure; holy shit.

After winding up my brief and predominantly awkward telephone conversations with Andy and Don, as they stumble through reminiscing about my first crazy little speech at the St Louis Club, as if that was the crowing achievement of my career, I had an uneasy feeling that my last big meeting wasn't going to be so enjoyable.

I somehow found it difficult to believe my two biggest supporters in the early stages of my rise to the upper echelon of the company now regard me as some sort of dimwit who lost his managerial skills somewhere along the line and really doesn't comprehend what he needs to do to set a good example for his employees; but it must be true; after all, they're getting that information from their trusty staff of spin doctors, who are smiling about the $5 or 6 million the company will save, knowing this will at least temporarily keep them in favor with the corporate power brokers.

Chapter 33
Completing The Circle

During the bizarre phone conversation I had with Rick Fish that late June afternoon, he cited a poor performance on my part at a sales training meeting in San Diego for being the catalyst for this next course of action, my pending retirement.

In reality, the events that unfolded in San Diego had nothing to do with the corporate hierarchy's decision to finally pull the trigger. It just gave them a credible excuse where none was needed.

However, there's no doubt my performance as a break out leader could be classified as "poor"; it was certainly irreverent as hell; so what else was new?

When I took a look at the very dry "sales training" material, I decided to make the bold attempt to add a little humor and personality to it during those dreadful breakout sessions. I misjudged my audience; these managers, who were mostly from Southern California where levity is frowned upon, generally didn't appreciate my fun-loving approach to dealing with the mundane and very serious business matters at hand.

As a result, my stand up comedy routine bombed in front of that shocked bunch of young managers; big deal, who hasn't bombed at least once or twice?

Also cited as horrible behavior in the San Diego atrocity, was my blatant and deliberate decision to blow off a dinner meeting with the likes of Rick Fish and company prior to the seminar. This one was ridiculous, but I had long realized that the truth matters very little when it comes to any recent allegations against me.

Of course I didn't want to go to that fucking dinner; but luckily, I had an alibi (or so I thought); none other than Jerry Dumas himself, the slightly hard of hearing guy in charge of the entire sales training seminar.

He told me it was perfectly okay to miss the dinner that evening since I told him I had about twenty tickets for the Cardinals-Padres game that night; tickets that I had blatantly and deliberately purchased weeks prior to this deal, which I was planning to use to take some of my managers out to instill good morale and all that other good business stuff; ironically, I bought all these tickets for the entire three game series way in advance of this meeting; a meeting that was originally slated for a Phoenix venue, but was blatantly, deliberately, and suddenly changed, less than a week before we were to go, without explanation; and that's a fact.

Without hesitation, Jerry said, "No problem; we'll get together tomorrow morning at breakfast to go over all the stuff."

Well, apparently it was a problem, Jerry.

I found it ironic that the guy from corporate; who assured me it was quite all right to miss that dinner, and apparently said nothing in my defense when the shit hit the fan (maybe because he couldn't hear what was going on), was a guy who corporate resurrected from the now defunct Enterprise Fleet Services, along with my original blatant and deliberate backstabber, Ernie Badger.

What pissed me off, at the time, was the fact that I had to eat twenty or so tickets to the second game of the series because we had to attend this fucking meeting. No regrets? I did have one after all; I should've gone to that second game, given the extra tickets to random people around the ballpark, and let those poor managers figure out all that sales training shit on their own. How's that for being blatant and deliberate?

I could just hear Jerry Dumas, while bellowing a speech at the podium, congratulating everybody for successfully making it through basic sales training, looking down at the commotion caused by my ragtag bunch of managers who due to my absence, were forced to learn how to sell on their own.

The spokesman for the group would be a guy named Zae, primarily because he had the coolest sounding name in that bunch, and a name that Jerry could never quite hear well enough to understand during the actual meetings; and that's a fact.

"What's your name, son?"

"Zae."

"What?"

"Zae, sir!"

"I still didn't get it; try one more time."

"I said my name is Zae!"

"What kind of name is 'Say'? Or are you asking me to 'say' something? I'm confused, but don't worry about that now; we've got a ceremony to get on with here. Where's your break out leader, son?"

"At the game, sir!" Zae's minions would follow suit, in decibel levels that would make Ernie Badger proud, "At the game, sir!"

At this point, an embarrassed Rick Fish would step forward, "Uh, yes

Jerry; these are Larry Underwood's people, and Larry uh blew out of here to watch the uh Cardinals play the Padres. Uh."

"So am I to understand that you learned basic sales training all on your own?"

"That's the fact, Jack!" The rest of Zae's minions would again follow suit, even louder than Ernie Badger himself could possibly roar, "That's the fact, Jack!"

Then, since they were clearly the type of go-getters necessary to handle just about anything, they'd be shipped off to Italy on some cool project where they'd get into some zany trouble, but ultimately, the unflappable Zae would hilariously and heroically save the day, and make the cover of the fictitious News-World Magazine in the process.

So yes; I'm here to tell you; that was my only regret; not going to that ballgame in San Diego, and seeing the Cardinals beat the Padres. But I guess you could say, I'm a lucky stiff; everything else turned out pretty cool in the long run.

When Jerry Dumas, our sales training general, still had responsibilities in the fleet services business working at corporate, one of his primary functions was to help get that business going, for any Group interested in opening up their very own fleet services department.

In 1999, I told Tim Welsh I'd be willing to do just that, brought on board a guy from Southern California, Kelly Hiner, to run the deal; and then brought Jerry out to give his presentation about fleet services and the opportunities it offered for our employees; since, after all, that was his job at the time.

As Jerry dutifully gave his presentation, his loud voice resonating throughout the meeting room at the Wild Horse Golf Course on Warm Springs Road, not far from my newly acquired bachelor pad where I would host many wild parties; I pondered how the company had come full circle in the quarter of a century I'd been working there. In the '70s, leasing was king, rental the redheaded stepchild.

The tables were turned, and now a guy who spent his entire career in rental, and whose promotion to General Manager was delayed due to the necessary lack of leasing experience; and when promoted it was under the assumption that the department formerly known as leasing, now called fleet services, wouldn't be a viable option for the Mid-Cities West Group.

But here we were, opening our own fleet services department anyway, just for the hell of it, to broaden the scope of my horizons, and perhaps develop some quality talent in fleet services who might even go on to become a General Manager someday; which of course sounds like a great way to end this book, but that was total bullshit.

Sure, that would've been great, but get real. Becoming a General Manager through fleet services was about as likely as some asshole like me becoming a General Manager out of daily reptile.

With that last bit of irony delivered, with a devilish smile, I look directly into the camera and give my last knowing nod and knowing wink, as we finally; fade to black.

Epilogue

I completed my active employment with Enterprise Rent-a-Car by 010101, remaining under a seven year "separation agreement", which paid me a little more money to stay out of the car rental business, send in quarterly updates to Don Ross, and not write this book.

My final visit to my deserted office on New Year's Day, 010101, was made as darkness had already erased the previously sunny and blustery Las Vegas day; to clean the rest of my personal effects out of my office, making sure the business related items were left in an orderly manner for my successor, Dave whatever his name was.

As I checked my inter-company mail one last time, there was a nice little, well scripted blurb from the cheerful President of Enterprise Rent-a-Car, Andrew C Taylor, addressed to all the employees of the company, thanking them for another great year, and looking forward to the company's continued success as imaginary glasses were raised high toasting the future success of the company, and then reality set in.

I was out of the picture perfect Enterprise world now. This carefully worded, politically correct message was intended for everyone still gainfully employed as a loyal and trusting Enterprise worker bee, not me.

The credits were rolling by as the scene had long since faded to black, but there was no mention of the starring role of the notorious maverick, "Uncle Larry", as himself.

I decided to send the President one last little farewell; in the process giving him my honest opinion of some of the things that rankled me in how his corporate underlings handled their mission of disposing of me. I waited until the very end to do this, so as to not disrupt the business proceedings of the company I was still employed as an Officer, the proud leader of the West Group, the Wild; Wild West.

His response was anything but heartwarming; nothing at all like the crap he had just dished out to the current faithful followers, and that was to be expected, I suppose; yet was so condescending it left a bitter taste in my mouth that would take a couple of years to come to terms with (only after a long letter to President Taylor which gave him the entire blow by blow job performed by Fish, the executioner on duty at the time of my whacking).

In perfecting the art of writing a condescending memo, strategic use of the words "disappointed" in conjunction with "comprehend" are excellent ways to achieve that goal. The recipient of the memo will realize that they caused the knowledgeable sender to feel "disappointed", and clearly it is because the recipient is unable to fully "comprehend" how they screwed up to begin with; thus, they are now proclaimed to be a nit wit.

With that matter still to be settled I was glad to see Andy's dad, Jack Taylor hadn't lost his sense of humor as I gave my final speech to an otherwise nearly humorless bunch of Enterprise Level 4 employees at my last Fall Officers Meeting, 2000. Most of all, I was glad I could tell him how much he inspired me, and how grateful I was that he gave me the opportunity to grow with the company, and for the most part, do it my way; which I think, fundamentally, that was also Jack's way.

The vast expanse of the West Group, which encompassed all or parts of six western states, would be carved up into a record breaking four pieces, as Arizona, Nevada, and New Mexico became new Groups, and good old Fresno became a part of the newly regionalized

Sacramento Group, which I (theoretically) had in my domain, along with Salt Lake City for about a day.

Darren Gottschalk and Mark Tobiassen were promoted to General Manager positions right where they were as Regional Vice Presidents, in Arizona and New Mexico, respectively.

Scott Kendrick didn't get the promotion to run the Nevada Group, and wound up making a lateral move to Sacramento.

The rest of the administrative staff either stayed put or shipped out to corporate or other Groups.

Whatever success I attained working for Enterprise, in particular, as the General Manager of the West Group, was largely attributed to the hard and often thankless work performed by the Group's wonderful front line employees; you know who you are; you were the ones keeping Jack Taylor's business philosophy alive and well throughout the Wild, Wild West.

Working with you was a joy, and I thank you.

An Ironic Footnote

Shortly after completing this book, in the fall of 2008, Enterprise Rent-a-Car began experiencing major financial woes. For the first time in the history of the company, thousands of employees, including 200 or so at the corporate office alone, were laid off, as this huge corporate bureaucracy had finally gotten too big for its own good.

Only a year earlier, Enterprise abandoned its conservative business plan of focusing primarily on the "home city" market, and perhaps unwisely acquired both Alamo and National; a move that is now being regarded as a dubious strategy, to say the least. The increased overhead and unwieldy operational structure seemed to be a large contributing factor to the huge losses the company started posting, almost as the ink was drying on this irreverent historical perspective of this once tremendously profitable corporation.

Many insiders believe this strategy will position this private, family owned company to finally go public, perhaps in another year or two.

In the meantime, thousands of disillusioned former Enterprise employees must try to find work, elsewhere, just in time for the Holiday season, as the company tries to keep the morale of its existing work force from complete disintegration.

These are the worst of times for Enterprise; the company that never laid a single employee off in its fifty plus year history prior to 2008; the company that I jumped over to when I was laid off from Georgia

Pacific in 1974 and desperately needed a job; any job.

In 2008, 86 year-old Jack C Taylor's estimated personal net worth was fourteen billion dollars. If he lived to be 100, Jack would have to spend one billion dollars per year to go broke, assuming that original fourteen billion dollar bounty somehow accumulated no interest each passing year; a virtual impossibility.

I don't think it would take more than a couple of billion dollars to pump back into Enterprise, to get them back in solid financial shape. I wonder if anyone in the Taylor family, or the extended Enterprise family considered that simple solution?

This final, ironic footnote on the company Jack built really has me baffled. Holy shit.

Printed in the United States
135538LV00002B/3/P